Variety Show

A collection of short stories and poems

Heather Richardson

Published by Heather Richardson
Publishing partner: Paragon Publishing, Rothersthorpe
First published 2021

ISBN 978-1-78222-871-4

Book design, layout and production management by Into Print
www.intoprint.net
+44 (0)1604 832149

I dedicate this book, with love, to all my family and friends who have touched my life in big and small ways.

God bless.

Variety Show

Introduction

This book of short stories and poems is the result of my love for 'creative writing'. The word creative being the real reason and writing as the means to express. I have written stories and poems for many years and stored them away. Covid lockdown gave me the space and time to gather them together and create this book.

Here is a little of my journey of how I came to write *Variety Show*.

I lived for the first 40 years of my life with undiagnosed dyslexia which should have put me off writing for good but I'm glad it hasn't. It's strange the way things turn out.

I grew up when dyslexia was known about but it was believed by many to be an excuse for bad spelling and not an actual difficulty.

I first became aware that others could do things I couldn't in my reception class at primary school. I could never hear the difference between the words three and four. For me it was sheer guess work as to which number was which and yet my friends knew. I remember looking round the classroom and thinking, how did they know?

I eventually learnt to know the difference and I carried on with school life. I knew I got things wrong and I thought it didn't bother me, when in fact it did.

My parents tried to help me. My mother bought me the same spelling book I had at school. I tore it up. My dad tried to help by doing dictation with me, I became cross and stormed out the room. I couldn't admit to my mum and dad what I really felt or put it into words but I didn't want to transfer my sense of failure and of being stupid, from school to home.

The eleven plus then loomed on the horizon. I never took it but my friends did. Instead, I was sent to the hospital to see why I couldn't spell. I don't think any reason was found. I was then asked to leave the school as they did not think I would cope in the senior school.

I left my friends and went to my new school.

In English dictation I used to get one out of ten and the teacher said that was because she was being kind. French dictation sounded to me like a pneumatic drill, I never knew where one word ended and another began, so I didn't score highly!

It wasn't until my sixteen-year-old daughter was diagnosed as being dyslexic that I realized I was at well.

When my children were growing up, I studied at evening classes and eventually went to the local Uni, where I did a behavioural science degree.

At the university I wrote my first assignment. To my dismay it was returned with no comment on its content but only how bad my spelling and grammar was. I felt I was back to square one and unable to get across what I wanted to say.

At this time, I bought a second-hand word processor that had a spell checker. This helped me greatly, but I needed to be close to the actual spelling of the word. Then my husband stepped in and offered to check my work and I thank him for all the help in checking and double checking that he did and still does. Now at last I was able to get my views and ideas across and I came out of Uni with a good degree.

A few years back I joined a creative writing group in our village library. Each month we were given a title to work on and at the next meeting we would read our stories to each other. This made me disciplined in my writing and many of the stories in this book started in this way. Due to a limited time at the group we had to make our stories short. This helped me to condense my writing and as you will find, many of my short stories really are short. Our writing group has helped and encouraged me and I say a big thank you to all the members.

I would like to say to other people who are dyslexic, you're not stupid, a failure or wrong. It can just take you a little longer to get there, I'm in my 60's! It is so important that you find a way to express yourself and develop your strengths and talents, many dyslexic people are very creative.

This book has been my chance to lay aside past feelings of getting it wrong and to enjoy the freedom to simply write. So, please excuse any spelling or grammar mistakes or if my poetry doesn't follow the rules.

Here for you is *Variety Show*.
I hope you enjoy.

CONTENTS

SHORT STORIES

POEMS

The Meeting

Fred had been eagerly waiting for this evening. He was slightly nervous as it was his first time. He pushed open the hall door.

A man was standing up speaking, "Welcome everyone." He looked up, "Oh here's a late one, come on in, don't be shy".

Fred nodded and took a seat in the circle of chairs.

"Now let's introduce ourselves shall we, I'm Peter."

One by one everyone stood up and said their name, a little bit about themselves and most added they had a drink problem. Fred felt his eyes widening, were these pigeon fanciers all alcoholics and why be so open about it?

Now it was his turn. Fred stood up, "I'm Fred Watts, I'm married to Mavis and I'm a keen pigeon fancier." He sat down.

"What have you forgotten to tell us Fred?" asked Peter in a kindly tone. Fred felt everyone was staring at him. "I'm not sure I know," he said.

"Well, it's your first time so we'll let it go for tonight," said Peter. Some of the group smiled encouragingly at Fred, whilst others glared at him.

"Now," said Peter, "this evening our group doctor is going to give us an illustrated talk, I will hand you over to Dr Susie York."

Good, thought Fred, now we'll get down to the real business, pigeon disease but why a doctor and not a vet?

Fred soon found out. The pictures were graphic and Fred felt sick as he saw slide after slide of damaged livers, in close up, from all angles. It dawned on him that this was not the pigeon fancier group.

He shuffled over to Peter and whispered in his ear, "Sorry mate but I'm in the wrong group."

Peter grabbed his arm and hissed, "Sit down, no need to make a scene. Stick it out man don't run from your demons; they will always catch you up." He pulled Fred down into the chair next to his. Fred sat. He felt trapped.

Dr Susie York was in full flow, she hadn't eaten since breakfast and had kept going on strong black coffee and a glass or two of vodka at lunch, as well as some in the wine bar on her way to the group. She thrived on the challenges in her hospital work but found she didn't understand the people in this group, but it interested her. In her heart of hearts, she thought they were losers. She had never failed at anything and she didn't understand their struggle. This extra work though helped pay for her expensive life style.

Her talk came to an end. Peter was back on his feet.

"Thank you, Doctor York, that was a riveting talk and shows how much damage we can do to our bodies, but it is never too late to change. We will now pair up and discuss with each other how we feel our bodies have been affected by alcohol."

Fred thought his moment of escape had come. But the young lady doctor was by his side. "Shall we pair up?"

"Sure," he muttered.

"Well," said Susie "how do you think alcohol has affected your body?"

Fred thought for a moment, "not in a big way, Mavis and I sometimes have a drop of brandy in our cocoa to help us sleep and special occasions of course."

"You are in denial, aren't you," said Susie.

"I don't think so," said Fred. "I just don't drink much. What about you?"

Susie was used to asking questions but not answering them. She gave herself very little time to think about herself and that suited her.

"Oh, I just have a drink here and there you know the normal but I'm here as a consultant. I don't have a problem."

"Nor do I," said Fred. "I came here to listen to a talk on pigeon diseases."

Susie gave an embarrassed laugh.

"You're a rare one," she said.

Just then Peter clapped his hands.

"Let's gather back together now and share with each other what we have learnt from tonight."

One by one the group members stood up to share their insights.

When it was Fred's turn, he stood up and said, "I have learnt that I am not an alcoholic and I never want to become one, if I have to attend groups like this." It was the longest speech he had ever given and with that he left the room and ran to his car.

Peter watched Fred go, he raised his arms in exasperation. "Some people can't hack it," he said. "I knew he was struggling from the moment he walked through the door."

When Fred got home, Mavis handed him a mug of scalding cocoa. "Had a good evening?" she asked.

Fred never one for much conversation said, "Different".

"Do you want a drop of something in your cocoa to help you sleep?"

"No," shouted Fred, "and I'm never touching that vile stuff again."

This surprised Mavis who said, "Ok dear, but you don't have to bite my head off." She tipped some brandy into her mug.

Dr Susie York returned to her flat where Rob her boyfriend was pouring her a large glass of wine.

"I bet you could do with this."

"True," said Susie downing it in one.

"Tough group?" asked Rob.

"The usual but there was one interesting guy who

was in complete denial," said Susie as she poured herself another glass. "I mean the length some people go to deny they have a problem."

She downed her glass and Rob poured her another.

Variety Show

Last Meal

I swept my wooden spoon across the greasy water and then felt around the shallow bowl. The only solid object was a piece of Cuttlefish bone. Tonight, my heart was beating too fast to worry about our cruel rations. I slurped every last drop and ate my wedge of stale bread. As I walked out the room fellow prisoners passed me their bread. I stuffed it in my pockets. This had to last me.

I entered our hut where the long row of bunk beds stretched down the room. Halfway down I tapped Fred's foot as I passed. He silently followed me. Fred was a guy with bounding energy. Even in this sadistic camp he appeared to bounce. He was cheerful, larger than life. As we neared the end of the hut, I saw that Sam was already there. Sam was desperate to see his young wife and their new baby. He was a good-natured lad. Being incarcerated was beyond his endurance. He wanted to be doing something, anything but mostly he just wanted out.

We were ready now. The guards patrolled the huts outside but could burst in at any time. With the bunk beds as a shield, I lifted the trap door. At the same time a commotion started at the other end of the hut. Two guards had entered. I saw Norris, the most inoffensive of any of us, a slight lad who depended on his glasses to see anything. He walked right up to the guards and stuck two fingers up. They turned on him pushed him backwards and I heard the thud of their rifle butt on some part of Norris's flesh.

We shot down the tunnel. Fred pulled the trap door shut and we crawled. We arrived at the other end and came up on the edge of the forest. We shook hands and knew it was every man for himself. I didn't look back but ran. I heard running feet, shouting and gun shots, I kept running.

After many adventures I made it home. The rest of my war was recuperating as my puny body responded to good food and freedom. I Knew Fred and Sam hadn't made it home but I didn't know what had happened to them until after the war.

I visited Fred's parents. I learned that Fred had been shot down and killed in the forest that we had escaped to. I wept with them. His parents wanted to know all the details of our escape and to hear about Fred's great love of life, right up to the end. They said it helped and I still visit them.

I also visited Sam's wife and bounced his son on my lap, which I knew he longed to do. He too hadn't made it. He had been gunned down at a checkpoint, when he was taken in to answer some questions. He had tried to run for it when the guard had left the room but he hadn't known guards were waiting outside the building. I was told he didn't stand a chance. I wept with Sam's wife at the senseless loss of a great guy and their future together. I'm still in touch with Sam's family and help out when I can.

I wasn't the only survivor though. I met Norris, purely by chance when we bumped into each other in London. He is now a city gent. He wears a suit that is too big for him and his glasses seem thicker than before. We beamed at each other and shared lunch. Norris had been a hero; he had single-handedly caused the commotion that allowed us to escape.

The guards had beaten him and smashed his glasses, damaging one of his eyes. I thanked him for his bravery. He said it had probably saved his life as he was so useless without his glasses, that he was put to work in the hospital wing and didn't receive the beatings the work gangs suffered. His body was so slight it is unlikely, he said, that he could have endured much more.

But I think he was being kind and I guess he had suffered greatly. When we parted, we promised to meet again.

I often experience survivors' guilt and realise the price my friends paid for our escape. Should we have bided our time in the prison camp until release came? Then Fred would be alive, bouncing his way through life. Sam would be home and able to be the great husband and dad he always dreamt of. Norris would have better eye sight. Only I had truly escaped.

At that last meal in the prison camp, I could have changed my mind. Then thinking of the Cuttlefish gruel and stale bread, I knew why I acted as I did. It was human nature after all. We had to fight back, didn't we?

The 'Beast from The East'

Tonight, I had lost my home. The tidal surge had ravished the soft sandy cliff and my bungalow had fallen like a house of cards. Then a huge wave had roared, swelled and crashed and my home was broken into pieces as if it was made of matchsticks. It should have been years until the sea claimed my home but the 'Beast from the East' had taken it and I could only watch.

Eventually I had been led away, passing camera crews and onlookers. I would love to have been just an onlooker. I used to love watching a storm coming in across the sea but now it was all over.

As I passed the path leading to the beach, I saw the lifeboat station being lifted up by the waves and its back broken in half. The power and force of the sea was incredible.

Now I'm at the pub with my numb hands round a hot cup of tea but for my whirling mind, there is no comfort.

The Barnes my neighbours are there, with their hands round mugs of tea. They have lost their home too.

We sit silently, for there are no words.

The emergency services and locals come in and out,

all of them are soaked through and look exhausted. I knew it wouldn't be long now.

Jack and I had bought our bungalow fifteen years ago. A new start for both of us. We had both lost our long-term partners and had high hopes of a seaside retirement together. It was only after the honeymoon period that I found out that Jack wasn't all he had seemed. He turned out to be a bully and a vicious one but only behind closed doors. He always acted as a kind gentleman when we were out or had company.

After eight years I had had enough and Jack left. The neighbours couldn't understand, they thought we were the perfect couple. I kept quiet.

The door opens again and in comes the police sergeant. Mr Barnes looks up, "Any news?" he asks.

"It's taking more of the cliff, the remaining part of your garden will soon go … and your shed. We've emptied what we can, and yours Mrs Silk," said the officer turning to me.

I mumble, "Thanks".

Mr Barnes gets up to go, "I'll help empty the sheds."

"No sir," said the sergeant, "You're better off here, we have saved and we will save what we can. It's dangerous out there."

Mr Barnes sits down.

As the policeman leaves, I get up and turn to the Barnes, "I'm not sitting here, we can't do anything. I'm off to my sisters."

"I think they will put us up here," said Mrs Barnes, "You don't want to travel tonight, and there will be floods and trees down."

"I'll be fine," I said, "it's only Lowestoft it won't take me long, I'd rather be with family."

I left hearing voices telling me to stay. But I couldn't.

The wind whipped around me and the rain blinded me as I ran towards my car, parked for safety behind the pub. It was as I was running that I found my way blocked by three policemen.

I stood stunned, dead inside as I heard their words, caught by the wind and sounding unreal.

"Mrs Silk, a skeleton has been found in your garden when the patio fell into the sea, we must ask you to accompany us to the station."

I stared blankly as they led me through the storm to the patrol car the 'Beast from the East' had finished me, my nightmare wasn't over. It was about to begin again; would I ever be free from Jack?

Variety Show

God's Moment

A moment in time
A second to glance,
To catch the essence
As if by chance.

Each moment is precious.
Yes, each one can be,
If we notice its existence,
What it is saying to me.

The moment when water
Is turned into ice.
The moment a bud
bursts open to entice.

The moment you touch
Someone's hand and just know.
The moment you understand
And love starts to show.

The moment a smile
Breaks the grip of despair.
And laughter erupts
As if from nowhere.

By moments we live
We have to let them go.
But to notice the moment
Is to learn how to grow.

Variety Show

A Christmas Bear

"Bargain of the day, cuddly teddy, a fiver." The stall holder held up a bear and waved it in the air.

"Ooh, put me down," thought the bear.

"I'll have him," beamed Mr Collins, "a fiver you say."

"That's right Sir, just a fiver." He took Mr Collins money and handed him the bear. "You won't find better in the whole market."

Mr Collins was pleased with his purchase and tucked the bear under his arm. He hummed 'Jingle Bells' to himself as he made his way home through the Christmas crowds.

When he got home, he shouted "I have something to show you." He held up the bear for Mrs Collins to see. "He's for our two gorgeous grandsons."

Mrs Collins clapped her hands in delight. "He's great, has he got a name?"

"No, I don't think so," said Mr Collins lifting the bear up to see if he had a name label on him. "Only this orange sticker on his ear saying he's a fiver."

"That's his name then," said Mrs Collins. "Fiver." And they both laughed.

Fiver felt very pleased, it was always good to know

who you were. He was happy when he had a hug, first from Mr Collins and then Mrs Collins. He was extremely fond of hugs and he was also very good at giving them.

"We won't want to part with him," said Mrs Collins.

"No," said Mr Collins. "The boys will only have him if they come here. We won't parcel him up with their other gifts, but if they come over this Christmas it will be an extra gift, otherwise Fiver stays with us."

"Good idea," said Mrs Collins.

Their grandsons lived an hour's drive away but they and their family rarely visited. John, the Collins's son and his wife Bertha both worked long hours.

Sadly, they didn't visit the Collins that Christmas or for the next three Christmases.

The Collins were disappointed but made the best of it, occasionally travelling over to their sons' home for a brief visit.

They became resigned to their invites for the boys to visit being cancelled because of some last-minute work commitment.

Fiver was happy though; he grew to love the Collins who were kind and generous people. The lounge which Fiver stayed in was warm, the television was often on and sometimes he was placed on the windowsill where he could watch the world go by.

It was on the fourth Christmas that John and his family visited. They came on New Year's Eve, with the boys now aged ten and eleven.

Mr and Mrs Collins were very excited to have their family with them. After a magnificent dinner, when everyone was settled in the lounge Mr Collins proudly picked up Fiver. "Look lads," he said "Look who is living here now. He has waited four years to meet you."

Fiver looked forward to at last being able to give the boys, (which he had heard so much about) a hug. The boys reluctantly looked up from their hand-held games stations and looked at Fiver.

James the youngest said, "Very nice," in a bored tone.

Sam said, "Not my thing." And they resumed playing with their gadgets.

"They have grown out of teddies and are past the cuddly stage," said their mum.

"What a shame," said Mrs Collins looking crestfallen.

Mr Collins gave Fiver a squeeze and put him back on the windowsill. "Funny thing," he said "but I never grew out of the cuddly stage."

The boys grunted. John and Bertha ignored his remark. They were going out to a New Year Eve's party and the boys would be staying with their grandparents.

"They will be no trouble," said John, "as long as their batteries last."

John and Bertha left the boys sitting on the sofa pressing buttons engrossed in the electronic world.

They grunted when Mr and Mrs Collins spoke to them. They ate their supper whilst still playing their games.

Fiver watched from the windowsill. He longed to be able to give the boys a hug. He didn't understand this age thing, Mr and Mrs Collins were older than the boys but they loved hugs.

At 8 o'clock Sam's batteries ran out. He then tried to grab James's game and the boys ended up wrestling on the floor. Mr Collins walked over, picked up both game consoles and walked out. He returned with a pack of cards.

"Try one of *our* games," he said. "No batteries required."

Mr and Mrs Collins taught the boys 'Gin Rummy' and 'Old Maid'. Soon the room was full of chatter and laughter as Mr Collins was yet again the Old Maid.

At ten it was bed time. The boys got up, Sam walked over and picked up Fiver. "He's coming to bed with me," he said.

"No with me," said James trying to grab Fiver.

Soon the boys were fighting each other on the floor.

Mr Collins parted the boys and took Fiver off them saying, "He lives in the lounge you will see him in the morning."

The boys both gave Fiver a hug and went to bed. The next morning whilst their parents were sleeping. Mr and Mrs Collins took the boys to play football.

When they returned it was time for the boys to go home but they didn't want to go.

"I have an idea," said Mr Collins. "You are old enough

to travel on the bus, why don't you come on the bus to town and we will pick you up."

The idea suited everyone. Every time the boys visited, they quickly lost interest in their electronic games and loved the attention their Gran and Grandad gave them.

Fiver wasn't forgotten, he always had and gave plenty of hugs. Now James and Sam are proud fathers and their children come and love seeing their great grandad, great grandmother and Fiver.

Fiver still sits on the windowsill and will soon be moving with Mr and Mrs Collins to their retirement home. He has lost some of his fur and is a little worn round the edges but like the Collins he has never grown out of the cuddly stage, which he is very grateful for.

Variety Show

Autumn

The garden centre must have known I was coming for it had a display called, 'First-Time Gardener'. There was a shiny dustbin to burn garden rubbish, a large contraption to hoover up the leaves, a fan shaped rake and a pair of plastic scoops to pick the leaves up. I choose the last two items. Rob may have them in the shed but as yet I can't face going through his things and the tool shed has always been his domain. I have never gardened.

Rob had died six months ago, suddenly and without warning, of a massive heart attack, whist he was cutting our lawn. I was devastated, we had been married for forty-two years. Since his death my son has cut the grass and tidied the garden but now, he is working abroad. I have advertised and tried to get someone to help but with no joy, so now it's down to me.

I came home with my purchases and came straight out into the garden. I lit the big pile of garden debris near the compost bins. First it billowed smoke, then some flames sprang up, followed by further clouds of smoke.

I moved away and with the rake I started to gather

the leaves. The leaves weren't all brown and drab as I'd thought, they were red, yellow and orange in different shades as well as some black leaves. I steadily worked around the garden, enjoying the feeling of my body being stretched, my mind free to wander.

The smell of the damp leaves reminded me of our firework parties that we had, when the children were young and one particular occasion which made me chuckle. Rob had lit an aeroplane firework which instantly flew off its perch and chased him down the garden, shooting out sparks and hissing like a snake. Rob was saved when he tripped over and fell, flat on his face. The plane flew over him and landed in the pond.

I wish he was here now and tears start to fall down my cheeks, I miss him like crazy. There is no-one to see and my tears silently fall onto the already soggy leaves.

Now I have filled three bin bags with damp, decaying pungent leaves. The smoke from the fire is blowing down the garden obliterating the house. I know my clothes and hair will smell of bonfire but I have always liked the smell, I think it's a healthy smell.

Raking around the apple tree, to my amazement, I uncover bulbs which are pushing up through the damp lawn, alive, pulsating and coming through the decay that's all around.

And as I rake by a border, I notice a dash of red, a rose boldly flowering, in the devastation around it.

I never knew there was so much to gardening. I had

found that it wasn't cold and boring, it was a living entity, dealing with decay and death by shooting new life into the drab world.

With an aching back I checked the bonfire, stacked my tools by the back door for tomorrow and brewed a strong cup of tea. Then I reached for the local magazine, where I had seen an article about a gardening club, they wanted new members.

If Rob is looking down, I think he would be amazed but pleased that I have now discovered the joy of gardening. It has shown me that I, like the tiny shoots that push through the dark earth, can work towards a new life.

Variety Show

Doing One's Duty

Prince Albert had been dead for some time and Victoria was hiding herself away at Osbourne House, still grieving for her beloved husband. She was in very low spirits only managing to do the bare necessities. The Prime Minister had been given the unenviable task to go and visit Victoria, raise her spirits and encourage her to resume her royal duties.

It was with trepidation that the Prime Minister arrived at Osbourne House, on a cold but bright January day. He was received by Victoria and they spent time on state business, which was completed successfully but to his annoyance, he had not managed to bring the reason for his visit to Her Majesty's attention. As he was being ushered out, he turned to her and said, "Ma'am I have a delicate subject that I need to discuss with you."

Victoria sighed, "Can't it wait until your next visit Prime Minister? Surely you can see I'm weary and have had enough for one day."

"I'm sorry Ma'am but it *can't* wait. It is a matter of national and international importance."

"Then you had better stay for lunch, and we can discuss it then."

"Thank you, Ma'am," said the Prime Minister feeling pleased he had at least broached the subject.

Lunch was a lavish meal consisting of several courses.

The Prime Minister didn't notice much about the meal as he was anxious, worrying how he could best approach the Queen. He did notice though that his plate kept being filled with an assortment of food and that he ate far too much.

As the dessert course was being served, he took a deep breath and said, "The matter I wish to discuss with you; that we agreed I would talk to you about at lunch, concerns your lengthy absent from public life, your subjects here and across the Empire are missing you, they and the government understand your terrible loss but—?"

The Queen raised her hand, "Stop there, without Albert by my side how can I be the Queen that the people expect me to be?"

"Your majesty, your subjects would welcome you back with open arms and the government would guide you every step of the way."

"Prime Minister, I do not choose this state that I now find myself in. It is the result of losing the one person that made me feel complete." Victoria dabbed at her eyes with a delicate lace hanky.

"Ma'am, I believe your spirits are low and that perhaps a change of scene to Balmoral or…?"

"NO," said Victoria loudly. "My home with Albert

was here and this is where I shall stay."

The Prime Minister's mission was not going well. The most he managed to accomplish was that Victoria agreed to a carriage ride with him after lunch.

"We'll go Prime Minister in the high wagon that dear Albert designed, you will be able to see over the hedges and enjoy the views."

"That would be wonderful, Ma'am, I'm sure you will enjoy the views too."

"I doubt it, I'm going so you can say to your cabinet that Victoria tried but nothing would lift her spirits, not even the best views Osbourne has to offer. Then perhaps you will leave me to mourn as I see fit. How can I laugh and be merry without dear Albert? The very thought" muttered Victoria.

The wagon was brought round to the front door and a small step ladder was placed at the rear of the vehicle; Victoria was helped into the wagon by two footmen. She squeezed through the half door and seated herself on the padded seat. The Prime Minister followed and sat facing Victoria. The footmen sat with the driver.

During the drive, Victoria sat stoically. She looked across at the Prime Minister. "Am I doing as the Empire wishes?" she asked him, with a twinkle in her eye.

"Your Majesty, the Empire and I only wish for your wellbeing."

"That is gratifying to know," said Victoria, "but I'm afraid I may be a disappointment to you all. All this outing is doing for me is upsetting my digestive system and doing nothing for my spirits."

"I'm sorry your Majesty, my digestion is suffering to, perhaps we should have waited a little longer after lunch, before taking our trip."

"Yes, dear Albert never paid much attention to the suspension and these estate tracks are bumpy."

They continued in silence until the Prime Minister suddenly stood up and made for the back of the wagon, "Your Majesty, I must ask the driver to stop, I feel indisposed."

"Oh, my poor Prime Minister. Stop driver," shouted the Queen.

The wagon came to an abrupt halt. The Prime Minister lurched forward he wrenched open the half door and leapt for the ground. But in his haste his trouser pocket became caught on the door's latch. There was a ripping sound and as the footmen ran round to the back of the wagon, they saw the Prime Minister suspended in the air, slowly descending to the ground as his trousers ripped further.

A footman unhooked his trousers which sent the Prime Minister falling forwards into the arms of the other footman, they both fell backwards landing in a muddy puddle. They quickly stood up; the Prime Minister held together his ripped trousers. He picked up his hat and cane which had fallen in the puddle. He felt totally dishevelled, he placed his hat on his head and could feel muddy water streaking down his face. With as much dignity as he could muster, he turned to face the Queen and found the wagon rocking and Victoria stuffing her hanky into her mouth, to suppress the laughter bubbling up in her, which was convulsing her whole body with mirth.

She managed, to say, "My dear Prime Minister are you all right, how is your digestive system?" Before stuffing her hanky back in her mouth.

"Fine, fine now Ma'am, thank you," said a flustered Prime Minister. "In the circumstances I think I and this young footman should return on foot to sort ourselves out."

Victoria nodded and between snorts of laughter said "Prime Minister you will be able to tell your cabinet and the Empire that you have momentarily lifted my spirits. I did not believe it to be possible."

With that she ordered the driver to move on. The Prime Minister raised his hat to the queen which meant he lost his grip on his trousers and they fell to his ankles. The queen could not contain her laughter and as he pulled up his trousers and the wagon moved away, he could see and hear Victoria roaring with laughter.

"Well," he thought, "I did raise her spirits but it hasn't raised mine." And he trudged despondently after the footman, back to Osbourne House.

Variety Show

Miscarriage

Bereft, left standing alone,
Torn inside, down to the bone.
Clenching emotions as they whirl around,
Blindly clinging to solid ground.
Disappointment abounds,
All is lost, not found.
Hopes and dreams dashed,
Promises and plans smashed.

Left is a trudge to seek new stores,
Of resilience, can you take any more?
Then the rejection of items not brought,
They were only a list, a mere thought.
They never had time to become real,
Hastily buried, so as not to feel.
Gone is excitement, possibilities, what ifs.
Life is emptiness.

With practical solutions some find their way.
But grief is grief and will have its say.
Anger, resentment, the silent scream *WHY*?
Followed by silence except for your cry.
Then time passes and fills up your heart,
Other things come in and play their part.
But depth has been added to all that you own
And the memory holds, etched on your soul.

Variety Show

The Power of The Media

Alf **parted the** laurel bush and stared across the immaculate lawn to the terrace. There in front of the manor house were the bride and groom, smiling confidently as the cameras flashed. Alf had been told that the groom was a well-known footballer and the bride a famous actress. But he had never heard of them.

He looked round at the rose arbour and the lake; all was well. His work was done, so he returned to his cottage. It was a still June evening but he didn't potter in his own garden as he used to. He sat. He saw no point in putting on the telly or radio. The clock ticked on. He could hear the wedding party in the distance.

Slowly darkness fell. Alf didn't put the light on. There was no point, for Molly wasn't there. Alf eventually drifted off to sleep in his armchair which he had done ever since Molly's death.

The next morning Alf was eating his breakfast when the kitchen door swung back and a young woman walked in.

"Hello," she said. And before Alf could say a word she added, "I'm Sandra from —" and she named a famous celeb magazine. "I've been covering the wedding and wanted to add a twist by interviewing some of the staff. Do you mind?"

And she raised her camera taking a photo of Alf with a spoonful of porridge in his hand.

"Brilliant," she said. "What a sweet cottage," and she merrily clicked away.

Alf never managed to finish his porridge, he was swept along by Sandra and found himself showing her round his cottage. She was shocked that he still only had an outside privy and took several snapshots. He told her his life story, she seemed really interested. He said how he had always lived in this cottage and how his father had been head gardener before him and about his life with Molly and how much he missed her.

Sandra scribbled on her notepad and snapped everything in sight. Then she shut her notepad and said, "I'll sent you a complimentary copy of the magazine," and with that she left.

Alf resumed his duties. He methodically did his work but he felt no joy. It wasn't until a month later that a copy of the celeb magazine landed on his doormat.

He picked it up and found the footballer and actress on the front cover and to his amazement an inserted small picture of himself eating his porridge. He couldn't believe it and quickly turned the pages. There was the normal glossy photos and gossip of all the stars as well as several pages on the wedding at the manor, followed by a double page spread about him!

He read it and re-read it not believing he could be in this magazine.

The article caught not only Alf's attention but also the public's, and soon local and national reporters, as well as TV crews, came down to film Alf and to interview him.

People started to come to the manor to see Alf and he gave garden tours. School parties came to find out where and how vegetables were grown.

Alf enjoyed it and found that he was missing Molly less. He slept back in their bed. He still talked to her. He chuckled as he told her "You'll never guess Moll but at last his Lordship has installed an inside toilet, the power of the media eh?"

And he leant over and kissed her pillow, before turning out the light.

Variety Show

The Secret Tunnel

2021

The *urban explorers* had found their way into a boarded up, ruined manor house. After exploring the ruins, they were now knocking out bricks in a blocked-up doorway. They were working in a room that had probably been the kitchen of the big house and they were eager to discover what lay beyond the blocked door.

1921

In 1921 the manor was an impressive family home. Anne, the daughter of the house, lay in bed staring at the ceiling. Tonight, was the night. Her heart fluttered with excitement and dread, would they, could they get away with it?

She had claimed a headache and left her mother and aunt in the drawing room, both sipping tea and waiting for the men to finish their port and cigars in the dining room.

Tonight, it would be the last time she would use the tunnel. The last time she would leave her room with a candle in her hand. She would never again creep along the hall to the red velvet curtain which hid the entrance.

She would never again take the key from her pocket, fit it into the lock and turn it. Then slowly and carefully so as not to make a sound, she would go through the door, locking it behind her and pocketing the key. For the last time, she would hold the candle high as she walked down the old servant's stairs, which led to the disused tunnel.

Just one more time would she run through the tunnel, not fearful of the dark, the cobwebs or the musty smell. Tonight, for the last time she would reach up for the key, hanging on the tunnel wall, which unlocked the door into the cavernous abandoned old kitchen. Then she would run to the outside door, which led to the disused laundry courtyard, she would turn the key and open the door. Ben would be waiting and she would fall into his arms, but this time it would be different, for tonight she would not be returning to her room.

Ben was her life, she loved him with all her heart. His parents farmed on the manor's estate and as children they had explored, discovered and played in the woods and fields.

When she had reached sixteen her mother had banned her from seeing Ben, saying, "She should consider her marriage prospects and not associate with farm workers." The rows that followed led her to verbally agreeing, that she wouldn't see Ben, whilst secretly seeing him.

She laid her hands on her stomach, on the gentle swelling and sighed with pleasure. To-night, she, Ben and their unborn child would be free.

She was ready. The grandfather clock in the hall struck midnight. She listened; all was quiet. She had already left her leather bag in the old kitchen. She looked round her room for the last time and crept out to meet Ben.

She went through the hidden door, down the stairs and raced along the tunnel, her heart pounding. She reached for the key hanging on its rusty hook, she placed it in the lock and turned it.

She opened the kitchen door and froze, for there was her mother holding Ann's leather bag. They stared at each other, with horror and disbelief displayed on their faces. Neither moved as time stood still.

But not for long and the repercussions were great. Ben's family were evicted from the farm and had to leave the district.

Life in the manor seemed to carry on as normal, except Anne was never seen again by the locals. It was said that she had gone to look after her great aunt, who lived in Scotland.

A few years later the manor was ravaged by fire, leaving a ruined building and the family moved away.

The manor was left to nature, ivy and brambles grew over and around the walls. There were tales of ghostly sightings and of a knocking sound which became frantic and then died away. The locals avoided the ruins.

2021

The urban explorers were knocking out the last brick,

which made a hole big enough for them to squeeze through. They climbed through the gap and found themselves in a dark, musty tunnel.

They gingerly walked a little further into the tunnel and shone their torches around the ceiling, walls and floor. Suddenly one man gave a shout and there on the dusty floor was a collection of bones and a skull and nearby the remains of a leather bag.

The police were called and the bones were sent for analysis.

It was discovered that it was a complete skeleton, believed to be about ninety to hundred years old, and was that of a young girl and a tiny baby. It was thought they may have been alive when the tunnel was blocked off, but no one knew for sure. The tunnel kept its secrets.

A Christmas Angel

It was Christmas Eve and the snow had started to fall almost as soon as Simon had left for work. He had rung at midday to say he was starting home as there was talk of road closures and more snow on the way.

Shortly after Simon's call Carol had felt twinges, which gradually developed into painful spasms. She called Simon on the landline but she only got his answer machine and she left a frantic message.

Then she called the hospital but the line was dead. "The lines must be down," she thought. Another pain ripped through her body. She picked up her mobile and saw her credit was low. She punched out a text asking for immediate help and tried to send it to all her contacts. The screen went blank.

Their cottage was a mile out of the village down a track. She looked out of the window, the snow was deep and still falling. She pulled on her coat and went to open the door when she was seized by a pain that took her breath away. She shut the door and returned to the lounge where she huddled down on the floor and wept. She looked up at the streamers hanging across the room and saw the Christmas tree and the angel on the top, in her pink dress and gossamer wings, the angels painted eyes stared out blankly.

"Help me someone, please help me." As another contraction tore through her body she gasped through the tears, "Help me, for God's sake someone help me."

Carol sat and let the pains come in waves through her body. It was getting dark. Then she heard the back door open. "Simon," Carol shouted in relief, "I'm in here."

"I know my love," said a woman's voice and in walked a tall woman. She was muscular with large feet and a large nose. Her face had a rash of pimples and she had facial hair on her chin. She wore an old-fashioned nurse's uniform.

"I'm Nurse Win, my dear, don't worry, I'll look after you."

"Thank you," said Carol in a small voice as another pain gripped her. Nurse Win almost carried Carol upstairs and bustled around making her comfortable and placing newspaper over the sheets.

"We don't want to make more of a mess than we need to, do we?"

"No," said Carol. She thought in normal circumstances she wouldn't have let this strange woman in, let alone let her tend to her. "How did you know I was in labour? I couldn't get through to anyone on the phone."

Nurse Win looked up. "It was a call from someone who knew you," she said. "They said you had called them."

"Oh, thank goodness," said Carol. "Someone got my message. Who was it?"

"Now let me think," said the nurse, "Ah yes, it was a nice sounding lady called Grace Harding."

But Carol had started another contraction and hardly heard what the nurse said.

Nurse Win helped Carol to concentrate on her breathing. "It will ease the pain," she said.

Nurse Win had a calming effect on Carol and although the labour was painful, Carol felt safe with her and as if somehow, she had known her all her life.

"Right my dear I want you to push now, use that contraction and push."

For the next few hours Carol used all her strength until at one-minute past midnight a baby's cry was heard.

"It's a boy, a Christmas boy, how lovely" beamed Nurse Win. "Christmas babies are so special. Now you just hold him, keep him wrapped up nice and tightly and I'll sort you out."

Carol cradled her son. Whilst Nurse Win efficiently and quickly tended to her and the clearing up.

"You'll do," said Nurse Win, patting Carol's arm. "I'll go and get you a nice cup of tea."

"Thank you," said Carol. "I don't know what I would have done without you."

"It's my job dearie," said Nurse Win walking out and quietly closing the door.

Carol lay back savouring the feeling of holding her

son in her arms. She heard the back-door slam and feet coming up the stairs two at a time. It was Simon, he burst into the bedroom and stood, struck by the sight of Carol with a baby in her arms. He then ran to her and his new-born son, he put his arms round them both and he couldn't stop his tears of relief and joy from falling. Together they marvelled at the new arrival.

Carol explained about just managing to get a message through for help and Nurse Win coming out. "She's making some tea," she said.

"Thank goodness she managed to get through," said Simon, "I have been so worried. I got your message but I couldn't contact you. I couldn't get through the snow; I have walked about four miles in snow drifts. I must go and find Nurse Win and thank her."

He went out and checked the whole house but there was no sign of her.

"How strange," said Carol. Then she was struck by a thought. "Simon, I have just realised something," and she clutched his arm. "Nurse Win said she came out because she had a message from Grace Harding, saying that I needed help. Grace Harding is my Aunty Gracie, *but she has been dead for four years!*"

"Don't be silly, you must have got the name wrong," said Simon. He looked out the window "But how did she get here, the lane is blocked by snowdrifts."

"I don't know I never thought to ask."

The mystery was never solved, no records were ever

found of a Nurse Win attending Carol on that Christmas Eve.

But Carol, Simon and baby Noel now have a new angel on the top of their Christmas tree. It is homemade and looks very similar to Nurse Win. All their visitors tell them that angels didn't look like that, but they know differently.

Variety Show

New Year's Resolution

Jan 1ˢᵗ 2002

I plunge the syringe into the soft sponge of the cup cake and push the plunger. I pull out the syringe and place the cake on the plate. I add a cherry to the top. It's very satisfying. I enjoy baking and the warm kitchen has set me thinking about this year's, New Year's resolution.

What should it be? I don't smoke or drink too much, I rarely swear, in fact I lead a very staid and dutiful life. So, it would have to be the same as last year I guess and that is, to be free. I desperately want my independence after a lifetime of caring for others. I want to do what I want.

Last year I had been caring for mum but sadly she died. It had been unexpected but her heart could have failed at any time. I thought I would travel the world with my inheritance but then Auntie Ivy became ill and here I am caring for her.

Jan 1ˢᵗ 2003

The door clangs shut. I'm banged up here for the night in Holloway. Hours of being on my own. If only Auntie Ivy's doctor hadn't been so thorough, I would have got away with it. He thought Auntie Ivy hadn't been ill enough to die so quickly. Stupid man, I just helped her on her way.

To add insult to injury I now miss out on my inheritance from her and after all I did for her. My siblings didn't lift a finger and will get the lot.

But at least this New year's resolution is easy, I want to be free.

Jan 1st 2013

For over ten years my New Year's resolution has been to be free and now I am.

Last August I was released early for good behaviour. It's wonderful to be able to do what I want, when I want. I had to move to Spain. The gossip at home was awful but I'm well set up now. I'm still short of cash for my grand plans, as my inheritance from mum went on solicitors' fees, now they are criminal.

I've befriended an old dear, here in Spain, she has no relations. She lives in a lovely villa close by. I'm baking her a batch of my cupcakes.

Push the plunger in, oh yes and my New Year's resolution for this year is different from the last ten years or so, it's not to be free but to learn from my mistakes, so a little less ingredient in the cupcakes. It will take a bit longer but the result should be perfect. And this time next year, well who knows, the world's my oyster.

Will Spring Come?

This poem was written in February 2021 whilst England was in lockdown due to covid.

Will spring come?
Will the daffs push through
And dance in the warm breeze?
Will children's laughter be heard
And crocus circles bloom?
Will the young green leaves cover covid's scars
And the birdsong rekindle life?
Will new-born lambs take away our tears
Healing our loneliness, grief and fears?
Will bright sun-lit days,
Make the dark take flight?
Will the human spirit soar,
As the gentleness of spring, appears once more?

Variety Show

Finding Mr Darcy

Andrew wiped the brass microscope carefully and replaced it in its wooden box. He sighed, straightened up and looked around his study. He was content with what he saw. Glass book cases full of large illustrated volumes. Then several glass cupboards with drawers beneath, holding his beloved specimens and on the numerous tables, tanks holding live exhibits.

The only blot on his horizon was his parent's nagging. They had hinted at it for years, but now they were saying that as he had turned forty, he needed to marry and produce an heir for Hagley Hall.

This morning his mother had said that she had come across a lovely young lady and she was inviting her and her mother for tea. Andrew had responded inwardly with a groan and outwardly with a grunt.

His mother took this as acceptance and told him he could show her some of his collection after tea, but added only some of them and reminded him to ask her about her interests.

Lady Fawcett's remarks were due to Andrew's past attempts at finding a wife. He had used internet dating agencies which claimed to match you with a likeminded person, but it hadn't worked. The first lady fainted when he excitedly brought out his collection of tarantulas and she had to be revived with a good dram of whisky.

Another had said that she needed the bathroom after he had showed her his numerous collections of beetles and other fascinating insects and bugs. He never saw her again. She had climbed out the bathroom window, tearing her dress and was last seen running through a boggy field away from the Hall.

Lady Fawcett had found this latest young lady at the last WI meeting. One of the members, Mrs Beeston, had brought her daughter Angela. Angela had looked sullen and appeared to be clumsy, spilling tea in her saucer and dropping cake crumbs down her front. She was twenty years younger than any of the other women at the WI and she was single. Lady Fawcett had seized the opportunity and immediately invited them both for tea.

Mrs Beeston was thrilled to be invited, she had never been inside Hagley Hall but Angela scowled, thinking how boring everyone was, there seemed to be no one her age left in the village.

She had recently returned to live with her parents after being made redundant. It was not by choice but lack of funds which had left her with no option. She was thirty-five and had always thought that by now she would be happily married, living in a lovely house with a brood of well-behaved children. Angela dreamed of finding a man similar to Jane Austen's 'Mr Darcy' but she had not had a happy love life and most of the time she had not had a love life.

Unfortunately for Angela she had inherited the least favourable parts of both her parents. She had her father's large frame, wiry hair and his clumsiness as well as her mother's thin lips, rough complexion and large ankles.

On the day of the tea party Angela reluctantly put on her best dress.

"You'll do," said Mrs Beeston. "You just need to smile."

But Angela didn't. She remained sullen and unsmiling throughout the tea party.

Lord Fawcett barked probing questions at her and Lady Fawcett watched her continually. This combination of interest made Angela clumsier and more awkward than usual and she dropped her cream and jam scone on the pristine white cloth, which embarrassed her and her mother even more.

Andrew hardly spoke. He was pleased when his mother suggested that he should show Angela some of his collections. Angela was so relieved to have left the claustrophobic atmosphere of the dining room that she gushed over everything she saw, including the tarantulas and Andrew started to see her in a rosier light.

He told her what a delight it was to find someone who shared his interest and how the other young ladies had reacted so negatively to his fascinating collections.

At that moment a light went on for Angela and an idea started to form in her mind, she enthused even more over each exhibit. Andrew forgot to ask her about her interests and raced from cabinet to cabinet explaining the delight, the near completeness and the exceptional rarity of his collections.

The afternoon tea had ended up being a success and much to Lady Hagley and Mrs Beeston's joy a courtship followed. This was spent bug hunting. Angela delighted over every creepy crawly that they found and Andrew grew more found of her with each find. When Angela uncovered a rare beetle, hidden under a mossy stone, that had been missing from Andrew's collection. He was beside himself and, in his enthusiasm, he asked her to marry him.

Angela's heart fluttered. For in Andrew, she had found her Mr Darcy, a landed gentleman, and an heir to an estate. She also realised that once Andrew was in his study and her future parents-in-law had moved to the Dower House, she would be in charge and the Lady of Hagley Hall.

Angela gave Andrew a radiant smile and accepted his proposal.

Tales of the Riverbank

Mrs Gregory lived in a thatched cottage, which sat in an isolated spot by the river. It had once been an 'Eel Catcher's' cottage. It was small, with pantries running off the main room. It had a corrugated tin roof on the lean-to kitchen, which leaked as did the thatch. Upstairs was the bathroom which had to be walked through to reach the bedroom.

Mrs Gregory set her own eel traps, she fished and grew as much fruit and veg as she could. She foraged for herbs and edible flowers and she knew the mushrooms and fungi that she could eat. To shop was a rare occasion for her. Sam Smith the gardener up at the big house, would often drop off some bits and pieces to keep her going.

Living close to the river was a joy to her, only spoilt by the pleasure boats that tried to moor on her private river bank. She would come out and shout at the boaters, threatening them by waving a stick, whilst shouting profanities.

People also passed on the footpath near her home and she had put up barbed wire fencing so the walkers had to pass in single file. She littered the riverbank and the footpath with notices, threatening prosecution if anyone came near. She was usually left in peace.

She knew the local birds and wildlife and which ones managed to rear their young and which ones didn't. She also offered first aid to any wild creature that needed it.

Today Mrs Gregory sat on a grassy bank near the river. She was waiting for her friends and she started to spread out the picnic she had brought. First, she scattered seeds on the ground, then choice leaves and grasses. Followed by plates of bugs and other plates with snails and slugs.

She sat back and waited. First to come were the birds and then slowly the other creatures came, a weasel, then a stoat, five rabbits, two foxes, three badgers, a couple of hedgehogs, a hare and a deer. She was pleased it was a good turnout.

She offered bits of her own sandwiches and cakes to her friends, some would come and eat from her hand. These moments were precious to Mrs Gregory, they made her feel content and at peace.

The first to leave the picnic today were the badgers, they snuffled off when they had eaten everything they fancied. The last to leave was the robin.

After the picnic Mrs Gregory was tired but happy and she went to bed early.

Unbeknown to her, at midnight an intruder entered her garden. It was Tom, a young lad from the village. He had been dared by his friends to take a selfie of himself outside Mrs Gregory's cottage as well as another snap shot of the inside of her cottage.

Tom had walked down the long lane to Mrs Gregory's cottage, he had been scared. He only had his phone for light as the overgrown trees blocked out the moonlight. As he walked the tree branches swayed above him and the grasses brushed against his legs and he couldn't help but recall the tales of Mrs Gregory being a witch.

He entered the garden and followed the brick path to the door. He took a quick selfie of himself by the cottage and put his hand on the door knob. He slowly turned it. To his surprise the door moved. He pushed and it swung open. Tom held his breathe but all was quiet. He took out his mobile and snapped a photo. In the flash of his picture, he saw many pairs of eyes staring back at him.

He screamed and ran.

Mrs Gregory woke with a start and grabbing her rifle, ran down the stairs. The door was open. She went outside and heard footsteps running away.

She screamed after them, "If you come back here again, I'll have you, you scoundrel, your nothing but scum!" Then she fired several shots in the direction of the footsteps.

She returned inside and scattered some biscuits onto the table. "There you are my lovelies, the last bit of our picnic. Now don't you worry you are safe here with me."

She went upstairs, brushed the mice off her eiderdown and got under the covers. She lay looking at the moonlight which struggled to shine through the cobwebs, which covered the small window. Soon she was asleep.

Downstairs the rats and mice were picking up the crumbs. Two badgers were snuffling under the table. A fox with a bandaged leg lay by the fire and a snake slithered from under a cushion, watching the mice intently.

Outside an owl hooted, a fox sent out a ghostly wail and young Tom lay on the overgrown track, he had been shot when Mrs Gregory had fired her rifle. His leg wound was pouring with blood. He fumbled for his mobile and saw his battery was low and in tears he punched the numbers 999.

Summer Frolics

I dreamt of a picture that was joyous, animated and surrounded by a glowing frame. In the picture buttercups danced amongst the long grass with Queen Ann's lace, ragged robin and pale blue forget-me-nots, all swaying in the gentle breeze.

Two young girls, one in a yellow and one in a blue sundress were picking posies. The blue sky with hardly a cloud in it, was dazzling in its brightness.

In my dream as I studied the picture it started to cry. Big tears fell from the top of the picture and ran in rivulets down the canvas. The different coloured paints started to merge together. I wanted to stop it, to keep the beauty of the picture and the sunlit days. I wanted to hold on to the innocence and safety of that time. But I couldn't. I could only watch, helpless to change the situation.

I awoke with a jolt. Where was I? At first, I thought I was at home and I would turn and see my twin sister Alice in her bed next to mine. But no, I turned and saw a Zimmer frame and a black wheelchair next to a commode.

I was here in this care home and I couldn't even get

out of bed on my own.

I couldn't wake my sister and run with her bare foot through the meadows.

I was dependent on the staff, on their timing, their agenda.

I felt sad, lost and alone.

"Morning Annie," said a carer, pulling back the floral curtains. "What a beautiful summer's day, do you remember we are going to the nature reserve today, won't that be lovely?"

"I'm sure it will be," I mumbled miserably.

"Come on now," she said, "we could gather some wild flowers and bring them back, they'll look fantastic." With that she bounced out the room.

Now here I am, like a baby in a buggy being pushed along a boardwalk between banks of wild flowers and grasses. "Can you see the pretty butterflies, Annie?" she said.

"Yes," I said, knowing my place, knowing the required response, playing my part. Together we picked a bunch of untidy flowers which I held in my lap.

"When's my sister coming?" I ask. "I thought she would have liked to come on this trip."

My carer stopped the wheelchair by a wooden bench, she sat down and held my hand. "She would my love," she said, "but do you remember she sadly passed away, four weeks ago?"

The shock had returned. I caught my breath, of

course Alice had a sudden heart attack and my beloved twin sister, companion and soul mate had gone, left me.

"I know why I had that dream last night," I said.

"Why, my love, what dream?" she asked.

I told her my dream. She patted my hand, was it a trick of the light or did I see a tear fall from her eye.

"We have to enjoy this summer now Annie and make the most of it, make the most of what we have."

And I know she is right. Back in my room as I place the wild flowers in the vase, I speak to Alice silently, "I know I must make the best of things but what is most precious to me are the happy memories of my time with you and our summer frolics together, throughout the sunlit years we shared. I will never let that picture fade."

And I place the last flower into the vase, a pale blue forget-me-not.

Variety Show

Your Place or Mine?

The dating agency had done everything it had promised. I had been given an introduction to Marcus. He was tall, dark and cuddly, a man who shared my interests, which included murder (the fictional type), eating greasy chips out of paper and Barn dancing. He had a good sense of humour and I felt we were kindred spirits.

That is until a few weeks before Christmas when I began to have doubts.

We were doing some Christmas shopping in a large department store and were weaving between the artificial Christmas trees and the displays of baubles.

I stopped and watched the flashing Father Christmas lights. "What do you think of those?" I asked.

There was no response. I looked round and saw he had moved away and was studying the book section.

I walked over. "I was talking to you. I wanted to know if you liked those flashing Santas."

"Flashing Santas sound creepy." He laughed and turned back to the bookshelf. "I'm looking for that Regency murder book, which your brother told us about."

"Don't buy anything for yourself until after Christmas."

"In the sales you mean?"

"No, you just don't know what will be in your stocking."

"You I hope," he said putting his arm round my shoulder.

"Come and see the tree display," I said, "its dazzling."

"I'm not bothered about that sort of thing, it's trashy, it's for kids."

"Well, I'm a big kid at heart, aren't you?"

"Not in that way, it's artificial, it's not what Christmas is about."

"I know but it's festive and it's our first Christmas together, I want it to be special," I replied. "I love Christmas, I always have."

"It will be special," he said, "I'm cooking, we will be at mine."

"No, at mine, I have it all planed."

He looked surprised. "What's the matter, I thought you would be pleased? I can cook you a lovely Christmas dinner and clear away, you won't have to lift a finger."

"That's kind," I stuttered.

"Great," he replied. "I promise it will be special, I want to give you a peaceful, relaxing Christmas."

"But it would be peaceful at mine and I was really looking forward to sharing Christmas with you, with the coal fire and a twinkling Christmas tree and stockings from Santa on the fireplace."

"I told you," said Marcus, "I'm not into all that commercial stuff." He walked on.

There was a frosty atmosphere between us for the rest of the day.

That evening I felt bad and I wanted to put things right. I rang him and told him I was happy to come to his for Christmas day and would he like to come to mine for Boxing Day.

"Yes," he replied, "we'll have a brilliant time. But Christmas only lasts one day for me. So, on Boxing Day we could go for a walk and have lunch at yours, but Christmas will be over and packed away until next year."

I put the phone down exasperated, perhaps we weren't so well suited. Didn't he believe in giving a little?

I did buy my tree and glittery baubles as well as a string of flashing Santa lights, which if I'm honest was to spite Marcus. I enjoyed decorating the cottage. I put the Santa lights round my front door so when he came round, he couldn't miss them.

I was pleased with the result of my hard work. But when I visited Marcus' flat, you wouldn't know it was nearly Christmas. His loft apartment was sparsely furnished and I knew he didn't like clutter but he could have had a tree and some stylish lights couldn't he. He didn't even have any Christmas cards on display. When I asked, he said, he opened them and shoved them in his desk drawer, which annoyed me but I didn't say anything.

At last Christmas day arrived. Marcus was picking me up at eleven. Right on time the doorbell rang. I grabbed my coat and opened the door. There he was holding a huge half cooked turkey in a baking tin, haloed by the flashing Santas.

"Would you credit it, there is a power cut and the whole block is without electricity," he said. "Can we have dinner here? I've brought all the food."

I looked at him. "You know it will include a tree, crackers, stockings, flashing Santas and the Queen's speech?"

"What a combination," he said, "I guess that is the price I have to pay to have a hot lunch."

We spent a cosy Christmas together toasting our toes by a roaring fire.

"Next year it will be your place," I said. "And you won't have to wear a silly hat or pretend you find the cracker jokes funny."

"Shame," said Marcus, "I've enjoyed it."

"Me too," I said cuddling up to him.

And it was a brilliant Christmas. Marcus did buy me some lovely presents but the best one I received from him was on Boxing Day. When we sat on his sofa to watch an Agatha Christie film, which he had recorded. It was at that moment that I realised something.

"Your electricity wasn't off yesterday, was it?"

"Why do you say that?" said Marcus looking uneasy.

"Because this film was screened yesterday from 10 to

12 and you don't have catch up TV."

"You've caught me out, Agatha would be proud of you."

"Why did you say it was off?"

"I realised I had been bossy and pushed you into coming to mine. So, I loaded up the car and came over."

I loved this man.

"Thank you. That was wonderful of you," I said.

"And next year we won't be at mine."

"Why not?" I asked.

"Because, if you agree, we will be at *ours*."

Variety Show

To Be

A path I seldom step upon,
Where wild flowers grow.
Where peace prolongs its stay
And there's everything you need to know.

A path where sadness is defused
Where happiness is allowed to bloom.
Where growth occurs and love is found
And you know you walk on Holy Ground.

A path I visit now and then
And wish I knew some more.
And It's there I'm simply me,
A special place, just to be.

Variety Show

A Cliff Hanger

The six lads slid down the steep incline. They pushed and shoved each other, calling each other names and bragging at how quickly they could reach the bottom. Douglas the youngest was at the back, he had to keep pushing his glasses back on and they were now as mud splattered as were his socks and shoes. He knew his mother would scold him but it was worth it to be part of the gang.

They all arrived at the bottom by the railway. "Ok Doug," said Simon, the eldest and the leader of the gang, "to be part of our gang you have to go through the tests."

Douglas looked up at Simon, "I know," he said. "I stole apples from Mrs Osmond's tree."

"Yeah, and she was in the garden," said Pete the second youngest. "You ran really fast Doug, I thought she'd get you."

The others chirped in boosting Douglas's confidence. "Ready for the next test?" asked Simon.

Douglas nodded, his stomach lurched inside him but he knew he mustn't let on that he was fearful, so he just stared blankly at Simon.

Just then a whistle was heard. "Get back everyone," yelled Simon. An express locomotive thundered past. Blowing their hair and clothes against their bodies. The blast of air and the noise of the express rushing pass, made Douglas step back and stumble over a lose stone, he fell down.

"You won't past this test if you're scared of trains," said Nick, Simon's younger brother.

The gang stood round Douglas looking down at him. "I'm not scared," he said. "I tripped."

He got up brushing off some of the grass and mud. Mum is going to be mad at me he thought, everything was clean on today.

"Ok then," said Simon "did you bring a penny like I asked?"

"Yes," replied Douglas, fingering the coin in his pocket.

"Right," said Simon. "To pass this test you need to double it in size."

"How?" said Douglas looking puzzled.

"You put it on the rail before the train comes, thick-o," said Nick.

"Yeah," said Pete, "and the train squashes it and makes it bigger."

Douglas felt a sense of relief, it sounded ok.

"We'll watch from behind those bushes," said Simon. "When you hear the whistle of the next train you have to put the penny on the line but you mustn't be seen."

Douglas looked around; the bushes were too far for him to reach if he was to place the penny on the line first. "How can I hide there's no cover here?"

"There is over there," said Pete, pointing across the track where the embankment went down to the river below. "Just place the penny and run across the track and down the embankment. We've all done it."

The other gang members bragged about what a close shave it had been and how you needed nerves of steel and did Douglas have it in him or was he just a kid.

Douglas looked at the older boys, "I can do that, I'm fast."

"Sure, you'll be fine," said Simon, "only time it right, place the penny and run."

Then they all heard the whistle. The boys ran to the bushes. Douglas placed the penny on the track with a shaking hand but it slipped off, he grabbed it and put it back on.

He looked up; he could see the train rounding the bend. He leapt onto the track and then went to leap off the track at the other side but he slipped and fell across the second rail, winding himself as he landed. He felt the track vibrating and felt the air buzz with the roaring of the steam train bearing down on him. Douglas froze and everything changed to slow motion, he was aware of the other boys screaming at him above the noise of the engine. Douglas saw the train charging down on him and —

Variety Show

Whodunnit

It was two weeks since the body of Sidney Rice had been found in the River Cam. He had been knocked unconscious by a blow to the back of his head and had drowned. The forensic team thought he had been killed not long before his body was found, possibly between 6 and 8 pm on the evening of November 26th. They also concluded that his body had entered the water near to where he was found, due to the movement of the river's currents.

When the police visited Sidney Rice's home, they found he had been living on his own and that he had an illegal stash of over 800 birds' eggs, some of them very rare indeed.

Chief Inspector Roberts was in charge of this case. He had already questioned Sidney Rice's nephew Bart, who lived on one of the boats close to where the body had been found. But there was no substantial evidence against him. Bart had said his uncle was supposed to have visited him that evening but he had never turned up. He seemed genuinely upset at his uncle's death, but was he?

Bart was Sidney's sole heir. The state of Bart's boat

showed he was in need of cash and he had recently lost his job. The Chief Inspector had also found out that Bart rented the boat from his uncle, who had threatened him with eviction, if he didn't keep up with his rent.

Another boat moored close to Bart, was a hide-out used by a cross dresser called Ray Slug, although on the boat he called himself or herself Rita Snail. He had also been questioned but he was more interested in his wife not finding out about his cross dressing than being charged for murder. There was a link between the two men though as they worked at the same manufacturing company. Could there have been a falling out?

The Chief Inspector had questioned some of the workforce but from his enquires he found that Sidney was a manger for packing and Ray was on the assembly line. Their fellow workers said that Sidney Rice was known as a bully but that Ray and Sidney had very little to do with each other.

Chief Inspector Roberts had also talked to Henrietta Rice, Sidney's estranged wife, who now lived in Sheffield. She had been separated from Sidney for three years. She was pregnant and desperate to marry the father of her child. She told the Chief Inspector that Sidney wouldn't grant her a divorce. She also said that he had been mean and neglectful of her throughout their marriage.

The Chief Inspector now knew that she had a reason to want Sidney dead but could she have come down from Sheffield and murdered Sidney? Would she have known that he was due to visit his nephew that evening? Her present partner swore he was with her at the time of Sidney's murder, both of them watching 'Four in a bed'. But could he be trusted?

Chief Inspector Roberts mused over the possibilities he really needed an eye witness; someone must have seen Sidney walking by the river on his way to visit his nephew. He decided to bring in the young woman, Miss Williams who had found the body.

Miss Williams had walked her dog later than normal that evening. She seemed very flustered and eventually admitted that in the past she had seen Sidney several times down by the boats. She hadn't like walking past him as he would wolf whistle and make suggestive remarks, so she had chosen a later time to walk her dog as she hoped to miss him. The Chief Inspector had quizzed her, to find out if anything else had occurred between her and Sidney. The girl assured him it hadn't.

The Chief Inspector wondered if in fact more had happened than she felt able to say.

The picture he had built of Sidney was of a selfish, bullying, crude man but he still hadn't deserved to die in this way.

He had requested a check on Sidney Rice's bank account and the bank accounts of Bart Rice, Ray Slug, Henrietta Rice and Mary Williams. The banks had been slow coming forward with this data, but now at last he had the accounts and he carefully studied them.

Sidney's bank account showed thousands of pounds coming in and going out. On checking where the money went out to, he found it was to an egg dealer in Hong Kong but it was where the money was coming from that really interested him. He now had a suspect in mind.

He had the suspect brought in and questioned. With the new evidence the suspect broke down and confessed all. He said he was being blackmailed by Sidney Rice.

Ray had been seen by Sidney when Sidney had been visiting his nephew. He had seen Ray dressed as a woman on his boat. He had recognised him as his male work colleague.

Sidney had come over to Ray's boat, laughed at him and ridiculed him. He had said they would be very interested about this at work. Ray had begged him not to say anything and sensing Ray's fear, Sidney had used it to start blackmailing him. He had threatened to tell Ray's wife, family and his workmates about his cross dressing.

Ray explained to the Chief Inspector that he felt compelled to wear women's clothes but he also felt shame and had never come to terms with his strong desires. The boat was his safety valve and when life became too much he came to his boat and became Rita Snail.

Not knowing what else to do Ray had, over time, transferred thousands of pounds across to Sidney. He was in a desperate situation with nowhere to turn and when Sidney called that night for more money, he saw his chance.

It was a cloudy dark evening with no one about. He had invited him onto his boat. As Sidney stood on the deck, Ray had pointed out to him a tree on the opposite bank, where he said an owl nested.

Sidney turned to look and Ray had smashed him on the head with a windlass. Sidney fell into the river and Ray pushed him under with a boat hook and held him there for a long time as he was scared that he would bob up, still alive. Then he had let the body slowly rise up and he had pushed it out into the current.

Ray sat before Chief Inspector Roberts a broken man. He signed his confession and was led away.

Chief Inspector Roberts shut the fawn file. Another case closed, another sad tale.

He sighed, for there was no rest for him as now he must get onto the Hong Kong authorities and stop the illegal egg stealing.

Variety Show

Hide and Seek

Sidney **looked out** of the drawing room window. The garden was transformed into a wonderland. A wobbly snowman took centre stage, surrounded by three small children, patting him into shape.

Sidney turned to Harold his lifelong friend, who was staying with him and Mary for Christmas, "They will be coming in any minute now."

"Making that snowman helped them get over the devastation that Santa didn't come," said Harold

"Yes," said Sidney, "I feel terrible. I can't think where Mary put them. We've searched everywhere."

"She certainly hid them well," said Harold.

Sidney sighed, how he wished Mary was here. The snow had prevented her from returning yesterday from her brothers. Now the phone lines were down and mobile phones rarely connected in this remote location. So, he couldn't ask Mary the desperate question, where were the children's presents.

Their three grandchildren aged from three to nine had arrived earlier in the week as their parents had won a luxury Christmas break in London.

Now Harold and Sidney had three children to

entertain and feed. The children had been inconsolable this morning when Santa hadn't left his gifts. To calm the situation Sidney had recklessly said that Santa was held up and there would be presents after lunch.

He and Harold had sat the children down in front of the DVD player to watch 'Mary Poppins'. Then they searched the house again whilst cooking a Christmas dinner of sausages, beans and chips followed by ice cream and chocolate sauce. No presents were found.

After lunch Sidney had to break the news that Santa still hadn't arrived. The children started crying and wanted their mum and dad and to go home. Sidney and Harold tried to mollify them and bundled the children into the garden to build the snowman. Then they both searched the house again and repeatedly tried to get hold of Mary on the mobile, without any luck.

Soon the children appeared in the drawing room looking dishevelled. Sidney and Harold pulled up socks found slippers and warmed cold hands. The Children eagerly asked if Santa had been.

"Not yet," said Sidney. The Children started to shout "We've been good why hasn't he come? We want Santa." They then started to argue over which child hadn't been good and had stopped Santa from coming.

It started to get physical as they picked on Alice, who had refused to pick up her toys on Christmas Eve.

Sidney was exhausted and wondered how he would manage and how soon they would go to bed. He looked at the clock it was only 2.30.

Harold saw the distress in his friend's face. "I know," he bellowed above the din. "Let's play hide and seek. You all hide, grandad and I will count to 100 and come to find you."

The children loved hide and seek and they eagerly ran off.

"Good idea," said Sidney as he started to count.

"You don't need to count whilst they are hiding, we can have a rest and find them in a minute," said Harold.

The two men sat silently by the roaring fire. Harold soon nodded off and Harold's snoring lulled Sidney to sleep.

Meanwhile the children had run round the manor house. There were great places to hide but they were scared to hide on their own, so they all dived into the cupboard on the landing, where the sheets and blankets were kept. The cupboard filled a deep alcove in the wall and went back much further than the children or Sidney realised.

They left the cupboard door ajar and waited. No one came. "They can't find us," giggled Alice. They settled back on some blankets.

"I want a wee," said Alfie the youngest.

"Just hold on," said Edward. "If you go out, they will find us."

"I'm bursting," wailed Alfie.

"*Shush*, go at the back of the cupboard then,"

whispered Alice.

So, Alfie did.

A few minutes later three excited children came careering into the drawing room. Sidney and Harold both woke with a start, "Just coming to find you," said Sidney.

"GRANDAD, ALFIE DID A WEE ON SOME BLANKETS," shouted Edward

"Why did you do——?" started Sidney when Edward interrupted.

"Look what we've found," and he pulled forward three pillow cases stuffed with presents.

"Where were they?" asked Sidney.

"In the very back of the landing cupboard. Alfie found them when he did a wee," said Alice.

"Three cheers for Alfie," said Harold winking at Sidney and he added, "Santa must know you like playing hide and seek and he hid them."

"Yes," shouted the children ripping open the paper.

Sidney and Harold sat back relieved. Santa had saved the day.

The Death of a Friend

S **am held the** syringe and stroked Ben's thick fur. Ben looked at him with pleading in his big soft eyes. Sam could ease Ben's pain with more pain killers but to what end? It was his quality of life that mattered and he had given Ben's owner the advice, that it would be kinder to put Ben to sleep.

This was the first time Sam had given this advice and as a second-year student his decision had been backed by the senior vet, yet still he hesitated.

*

His mind went back to a warm June day, when he was twelve. He should have gone for the school bus but instead he had run down the sandy path, behind their house, to the deserted shingle beach, where he had thrown himself down and wept. Tears that tore through his body. Tears that expressed his heartbreak of losing Charlie his soulmate.

Charlie, a golden retriever had protected Sam, ran with him, shared his joys and his sorrows, loved and accepted him. Now he was gone. In the night when Sam was asleep, Charlie had started to vomit blood and his condition had deteriorated. His father had rushed Charlie down to the emergency vet but there was nothing they could do; Charlie had a massive heart attack and he had to be put to sleep.

Through his tears Sam heard footsteps crunching on the shingle. He looked up and saw his mum coming towards him. He started to get up to run, for he was not going to school today, whatever his mum said. He ran down the beach. He turned to see how close his mum was but she was sitting down on the shingle.

So, he turned and went to join her. She put her arm round him. "Fifteen years we had old Charlie boy, older than you. He's always been there, hasn't he?" She said, looking out towards the placid sea.

"Yes" whispered Sam. As more tears fell.

His mum held him tighter and they sat together allowing themselves to feel the loss of their beloved friend.

Charlie had been the reason Sam had become a vet. He had had other wonderful dogs but none had touched the spot that Charlie had in his heart.

*

Sam now looked back at Ben's owner, Mr Jackson, a middle-aged man, who was reassuring Ben with tears in his eyes. Sam thought back to his lectures, he heard Mr Prices booming voice saying, be calm, professional and quick, don't prolong the agony. Sam plunged the syringe in. He watched Ben's eyes that slowly showed life was draining from him. He tested for a pulse or heartbeat. He said and did the necessary things and the nurse took Mr Jackson out.

Sam knew his next patient was waiting but he felt like his twelve-year-old self, he wanted to run but he moved Ben into the back room and swabbed down the counter, wiping the tears away. He promised himself a large glass of wine at the end of his shift. He opened the door and called in his next patient, a cheeky hamster, who needed his nails cutting.

Before the following patient. The nurse returned with a strong coffee for Sam she patted his arm and said, "Well done, you'll make a great vet, you said just the right things."

"I had a good teacher," said Sam, "he taught me a lot; he was called Charlie."

Sam smiled to himself for he realised he had just overcome his greatest fear about becoming a vet.

Variety Show

Make Do and Mend at Christmas

War was declared in September last year and it wasn't over by Christmas as they had told us. Last year Cyril was still home but in April his call up papers came and he's now finished his training and waiting in camp to be sent to, who knows where.

So, it's just me this Christmas. Cyril said I must be strong for the children, Mattie and Beth. I'm trying but the rationing is getting worse and with all the queuing and scrimping and saving it makes my nerves jangle. The bombing scares me. I sit in the underground hugging the children. What sort of childhood is that for them?

But I'm doing my best. We're getting ready for Christmas, Mattie and Beth have painted newspaper to make paper chains. Mattie chose black, goodness knows why and Beth yellow. So, our front room will look like a bee hive by the time they have finished.

I've been dreading finding them presents, there is nothing to be had unless you can afford the huge prices they are asking. But I've managed to make Beth a doll out of Cyril's old socks. And my dad has made Mattie a train engine from scraps of wood. Then for their stockings I've got them a comic book each and some cardboard cut-out animals, plus a colouring book. Of course, there's no colourful wrapping paper, so newspaper will have to do.

I've delivered all the Christmas cards, but they are so flimsy I doubt they will stand up on the mantelpiece. Still, it's the thought that counts.

As for Christmas dinner, well, that had me scratching my head but I've decided, carrot soup, if there's nothing else there is always carrots. Then rabbit with parsley and celery stuffing, I know it sounds posh but my sister had it at a friend's house and said it was tasty and easy to make. She sent me the recipe. With it we will have Carrots again and cabbage, potatoes of course with gravy and bread sauce. I'm getting hungry just thinking about it.

For pud I'm making a ministry of food recipe *'eggless Christmas pudding*. Don't know how that will turn out. I'm saving my coupons up for everything and asking mum and dad for theirs as they are coming for Christmas.

It's now Boxing Day and it's over. It was grand. The children had their stockings at first light. Mum and dad came. Mum helped me with the cooking, whilst dad played with the children. The dinner was tasty, even if I say so myself. The eggless pudding was surprisingly good but crumbly. It was all washed down with dad's peapod wine; it was strong stuff.

Then we opened our presents, the kids loved theirs. Mum and dad gave me a pretty apron that mum had made. I gave dad a couple of bottles of his favourite brew and I'd embroidered some hankies for mum, with her initials on, she was chuffed.

We listened to the Kings speech on the wireless. Dad insisting that we all stood to listen. I still can't get over the fact of hearing the king's voice.

We finished the day with a good old sing song round the piano.

So, Hitler you tried but you didn't manage to spoil our Christmas. Just wish Cyril had been with us, hopefully he will be next Christmas and this war will be over.

Conflict

Should I be like you,
Or should I be like me?
A rose is not a buttercup
And never meant to be.

You're strong in ways I want
And I've depths you do not know.
Your ways are more conspicuous,
Your ways are more on show.

My ways are ways of quietness
And reflecting what I find.
To watch and understand,
To take a quieter line.

Others swim in noisy waves.
I flounder out my depth,
Afraid to let them know
I'm pulled beyond my breadth.

Don't push me so I lose,
All thoughts of who I am
And decide I should be,
A different type of man.

Christ's body is made of many parts.
We're a variation of a theme.
Let's each own our uniqueness,
To be used in God's perfect scheme.

Variety Show

Spit Spot

It **rained and** rained and rained. It lashed against the window pane and made our front garden a quagmire. It didn't matter, nothing mattered. I was in turmoil. Last night he had left me to move in with Veronica Blunt.

Veronica with her big goofy glasses, long flowing skirts and sandals, which she wore in all weathers. People laughed at her behind her back. Her hair was grey, long and straggly and my husband had moved in with HER. Moved into her scruffy, peeling, shanty cabin on the shingle spit.

He had left me and our four children, he had left our immaculate four-bedroom house for a tumbled down wooden beach hut.

I hadn't slept but I'd got up at my normal time, I had done my aerobic exercises, cooked lasagne for tea and sorted out my cosmetic deliveries for the week. Now I needed to wake the children, get breakfast and do the school run. I had to keep it normal for the girls, as I'd told them he had been called away for work. I couldn't manage their upset; how could I explain.

I got the children to school. Then I came home and

sat. What was I to do, what was I to say? What did he see in her?

The phone rang and it was him. I screamed obscenities at him and slammed the phone down. Ten minutes later I rang him, I needed to know. His answers left me stunned. I thought we shared the same ideals but no.

When I asked him what it was that attracted him to Veronica?

He replied it was her inner beauty.

I'd said, "don't I have inner beauty?"

He said, "of course but it's not the same and that he wanted his freedom, he wanted to get back to nature, not to be always meeting deadlines and never having the time to be in 'the moment'."

What could I say to that? I'd worked hard to build our family, to buy nice things, as had he. I had helped him to climb the ladder as well as working and looking after the house and children.

He said, "we want different things, you want perfection and I don't, I want to be creative."

I said "leaving me to be with Veronica Blunt is very creative as I could never have imagined such a thing, not even in my wildest dreams."

He said, "you don't dream enough."

I then hung up. I couldn't listen to any more. Here I am, I take care of myself I have a good figure. Veronica doesn't even wear a bra; she boils seaweed and knits with rope, washed up on the shore. How can I tell anyone that he had left me to be with her?

One of the mums at the school this morning, said that the spit was getting flooded, as it sometimes did and then it would also flood the shanty village as it's in a dip, to protect it from the north easterlies.

Perhaps he will come home dripping wet and want a bath and a fluffy laundered towel. He would get dry clothes from his wardrobe, where his clothes are colour coordinated and pressed beautifully, by me.

*

But he didn't come home that day or the next and it is now ten years since he left me. I'm now the 'organisational executive' of the nuclear power station, which is situated on the spit. I'm also married to the power station's chief executive and we live in a mini mansion on the edge of the marshes.

The children have all done well and are starting out with good degrees, except for Sophia who now lives with her dad and Veronica in the shadow of the power station, still in the shanty cabin. They have a small business producing what they call 'sea art', made from material washed up on the shingle.

I met him the other day as I was inspecting the perimeter fence of the power station.

He asked me if I was happy and said he hoped I was.

I replied, "I'm happy enough, I should be as I want for nothing except for more time and how about you?"

I asked, "are you happy?"

He replied by opening his arms to encompass the shanty village and shingle spit, "how could I not be?"

I raised my eyebrows, "I'll never understand," I said.

"No," he said, "I guess you won't."

The easterly wind blew our hair and clothes, we had to brace our bodies against it. We stood staring at each other. We had shared so much, shared the same environment, lived and worked on this narrow spit. Yet we were miles apart and there was now no common ground between us.

I turned and walked away. Meeting him had left me feeling incomplete, as if I had missed something important. Bizarrely that feeling is still with me.

The Delivery Man

It was early dawn; Tim woke with a start; it was foggy and wet. He knew he had a lot to do. He pushed back the covers trying not to disturb Carol. She stirred, then started to snore again. Tim breathed a sigh of relief; Carol was a good sort but she fussed too much. He got dressed pulled on his boots and went down to make porridge.

He hummed a merry tune as he mixed his porridge oats with milk. He mentally went over all he had to do, as long as he was organised, he would be ok. First, he must see to the animals. He swilled his porridge bowl and walked out into the foggy drizzle which made everything damp and dreary.

He mucked out and fed all the animals. He knew each one by name and he loved each one of them as they did him. There was a warmth in the stables and he would love to have stayed but he needed to check his new purchase, a state-of-the-art delivery vehicle, especially streamlined for speed.

Carol worried about Tim's love of fast transport. Tim had to keep explaining that he needed it for his work. Carol didn't always appreciate the importance of his job.

He took a cloth and loving buffed up the upholstery and shiny exterior. Later it would be brought to the factory to be used for the very first time. Again, he would like to have stayed longer in the garage but he must get to work.

Carol and Tim worked at the same factory. Carol did the late shift in the canteen. Tim's main job was as a delivery driver but he had a hand in most of the areas, helping wherever he was needed.

When he arrived, he heard the sound of hammers on wood, the clang of metal being beaten into submission and he smelt paint mixed with the smell of glue. He entered the building and was immediately called upon to help with this and that.

Then he went to the dispatch area and sighed over the long list of deliveries that would need to be made. It was excellent that orders were always coming in but it worried him about meeting the promised deadlines.

Time passed quickly and soon it would be getting dark. A loud bell rang. The factory became silent.

"All hands to load up," shouted the foreman. Soon the courtyard was busy with everyone helping to load up Tim's new delivery vehicle.

Then Carol came out of the canteen with a tray of mulled wine. Everyone took a glass and looked expectantly at Tim. Tim kissed Carol got into the delivery vehicle and raised his glass, "Merry Christmas everyone," he said, as the sleigh stared to move, pulled by the reindeer. Soon they were flying high in the sky.

Beneath him Carol and the factory workers waved and cheered.

As they soared higher Tim felt his fears and worries fade, this was what he loved and as every year before, he would deliver to every child and meet his targets on this special night. With that thought he urged his reindeers to go even faster.

Variety Show

Lost

The hedges were thick. I couldn't see through them, but I could hear the voices of my family calling. At first it was Jason my four-year-old son who called, "Mummy, Mummy where are you?"

"I'm here Jason," I replied, "I'll come and find you."

Then Mark my husband's voice, "Sindy, we are in the centre, we will wait for you."

Then my dad who had passed away ten years ago, "This way Sindy come on, you can do it."

And then others voices blurred together making no sense, some of the voices were kind and others threatening.

I ran on through the maze and at last I reached the centre but there was no one there.

I heard Mark shout, "Over here Sindy, we are making our way out."

But I couldn't see anyone. The other voices came back jeering at me and telling me I was useless. I covered my ears to block the sound but it didn't stop. I crouched on the ground and sobbed.

Then I heard a different voice, "Sindy what are you doing out of bed. Come on dearie up you come." I felt arms under my arms helping me up.

I opened my eyes. "Where's the maze, where's Jason?" I asked looking at a blank pale blue wall.

"There's no maze, Sindy and Jason's at home, you're in hospital and you had a bad dream. Now jump back into bed."

And I did. Then the nurse left, turning off the light. Immediately the voices started again and I dare not close my eyes in case I would find myself back in the maze, with no way out.

So, I remained for the rest of the night lying rigid beneath my hospital blankets.

At six a nurse came in with a cup of tea. "Rise and shine, it's a lovely morning." She beamed.

"Is it?" I asked.

"Yes, and you had a good night last night, nurse Haines said you were only disturbed once in the night. That's the best night you've had. Those new tablets must be working."

"No, it was terrible I was lost in a maze and I couldn't find Jason …"

But before I could finish, her bleep went off and she ran out. Shouting behind her, "Don't worry you are doing well, you'll soon be home."

I stared at the pale blue walls. I wasn't sure why I was here but I remember home and it had been a terrifying place, the voices came out of the walls there and nowhere was safe. Here at least the walls didn't speak. I found some comfort in that thought.

Maybe, I thought if they keep me here long enough, I might find my way out of the labyrinth and back to being me, whoever that is.

Variety Show

Mary And Martha

I clean the hearth and sweep the floor,
There's a knock at the door.
"Could I have coffee with you this morn?"
We sat together comfortably,
You told me of Your love for me
And I responded tearfully.

You told me how You wish to be with me
And spend time alone, just us.
The warmth of Your love invaded the room.
The peace of Your presence soothed my hurried mind.
You didn't mind if we drank coffee or wine,
You just wanted my time.

In peace we sat just listening.
Then silence came and I was filled with You.
The time passed and I received.
I knew You didn't want to leave.
But there's lunch to get
And beds to make.

But my special time was with You,
Please, come again soon.

Variety Show

Three Have an Adventure

I looked at the ten-year-old twins Jo and Jim, they were mine for the day. "Well," I said, "shall we go and find where the smugglers hide out?"

The boys erupted into joyous whoops and ran round jumping on and off the sofa.

Their grandad who was trying to read said, "Take them out for goodness sake, let me have some peace."

I picked up the picnic basket and we drove the short distance to Landlow inlet. A naturally sheltered harbour for small yachts. The sun blazed down and little boats bobbed on a deep blue sea, with a bright blue sky above. The inlet was surrounded by woods, which in places were ablaze with rhododendrons. The woods came right down to a sandy shore, where the boys loved to swim, make sandcastles and bury their grandfather but today we were doing none of these things, we were off on an adventure.

I had borrowed my friend's rowing boat and we were going to search for smuggler's. The boat was a large battered, wooden rowing boat, with peeling red paint. The boys jumped in and the picnic hamper was stored under the front seat. I pushed the boat into the water, then jumped in. We were off.

The boys took an oar each and we went round and round in circles, until I took one oar and the boys took it in turns to partner me. We explored the little creeks that branched off the inlet, then on the banks of one creek we found a derelict cottage. We tied the boat to an overhanging branch and started to explore. The cottage door swung on its rusty hinges and we entered into the dark interior.

We had soon explored the four small rooms and the lean-to kitchen. We had our picnic in the front room of the cottage. The boys expected smugglers to appear at any moment, luckily, they didn't. We were packing up when Jo spotted a trap door cut into the floorboards. The boys raced to it and pulled the iron handle. It gave, then fell back shut. It took the three of us to pull it right back. There were steps leading down.

On the top step was a half-burnt candle. The boys found some matches by the old stove. I lit the candle and led the way down the steps. It became colder and a musty smell rose up. Then we were in a small room with stone ledges around it and on the ledges were racks of bottles. Jim picked two bottles up. At that moment the candle went out and the boys raced back up the steps, quickly followed by me.

The bottles appeared to be a French wine. To me it looked like cheap plonk but the boys were delighted and thought they had found the smugglers hoard. I didn't think it would matter taking the two bottles with us. I left a £10 note on the top step and we shut the trap door.

We rowed back and made our way home.

When my daughter arrived for tea. We opened the smugglers wine, which turned out to be very potent. The boys and their mum had to stay the night as our daughter, who had only drunk two glasses, was soon asleep and snoring on the sofa.

The wine had even mellowed grandad who tucked the boys up in bed and read them a 'Famous Five' adventure, whilst finishing off the wine.

"We have better adventures than them," said Jim.

"Yes, we do," said Jo. "We found a real smugglers hoard didn't we grandad?"

"It was a good day's work," slurred grandad as he stumbled out of the bedroom holding the empty bottle, with a silly grin on his face.

"Smugglers make grandad very happy, don't they?" said Jo.

"Yes, he must love them as much as we do," said Jim, snuggling down under the covers.

And soon the whole family were fast asleep.

Variety Show

River Talk

My feet felt the refreshing coolness of the water as I sat on a boulder in the middle of the shallow, rock strewn river. I sat, overcome by the remoteness and grandeur of the scene around me. Wooded cliffs rose from the banks of the river and in some places rugged cliff faces dominated. Lichen and moss clung to the tree branches, the trees in turn clung to the rocks.

I revelled in the beauty of solitude as the sun penetrated this oasis with dappled sunlight beneath the trees and direct sunlight on part of the water, the water responded breaking into a myriad of colours. Where the sunlight caught the boulders, they lost their harshness and appeared warm and yielding.

Sitting I listened and in the gushing and rushing of the water I thought I heard children's laughter. I pictured them with rolled up trousers, screaming, splashing and jumping from boulder to boulder. Their parents enjoying their children's joy and freedom.

I listened again and the water rippling by brought with it the sound of a fisherman, pulling out of the river a splashing trout. The fisherman grunted with the effort of getting the fish into his net. I felt his satisfaction, his contentment in waiting and his sense of achievement.

Then I picked up a different sound. I heard a roaring sound, a pounding vibration. I started to rise to leave my spot but as I looked around all was well. It was the river speaking to me. I heard the smashing of boulder upon boulder and in my mind's eye I saw the fury of the river, in full flood, charging to the sea taking all in its path.

The villagers heard it too, on that night long ago and soon screams joined the roar as the river spewed boulders into cottages and villas. It broke them, tore them, taking the young and the old. I heard the screaming and covered my ears there was nothing I could do but listen to the river and nothing the people could do, to stop the torrent.

Yet was that macabrely part of the river's beauty. Man couldn't tame it, it was wild and unruly, giving in season and taking in season, oblivious to man, its beauty untouched.

I rose to go but the river had one more thing to tell me. In the gurgle as water plunged between two stones, it told me that I would return again and again, that I was under its spell and I knew without a doubt, the river was right.

The Diary of Fred Barnes Aged 87 and 3 Months

Jan 1st

Hello diary, it's a brand-New Year.

My New Year resolution is the same as my brothers and that is that we should get on with each other. We have both had this resolution for 77 years. Our mum made us make it when we were nippers as she was fed up with us squabbling, but neither of us have kept it for more than a few days.

Sid is my elder brother by two years so by rights it should be Sid going into a home but my legs have given up on me and I need help to get around.

Sid helps when he feels like it but a lot of the time he can't be bothered. We have never been close but after mum died things between us became more difficult. Mum left the house to both of us.

We both wanted to move back into the family home and neither of us would back down. So, we split the house. We both ended up with our own bedroom and lounge and shared the bathroom and kitchen, where we had a fridge each and designated cupboards. We also split the garden, that was easier we put a fence straight down the middle.

As two confirmed bachelors we managed ok, mostly by ignoring each other. Now my legs have packed up and Sid gets fed up with helping me and I hate asking him.

Mrs Oslo a 'do-gooder' has arranged for me to try out St Peter's home.

I know I need help, so I'm giving it a trial period.

Jan 2nd

I Moved into St Peter's today. Sid couldn't wait to see the back of me, he virtually pushed me out the house and I gave him a mouthful, so I guess we have broken our New Year's resolution already.

St Peter's seems warm and homely. Too tired to write any more.

Jan 9th

I have been at St Peter's one week and I like it. My room is bright and large, with my own ensuite. The staff are kind and don't snarl at me when I ask for help as Sid did. The food is great, better than my microwave meals. Best of all Tim Hopkins is here, we were at school together. He's still got all his marbles so we have had a good laugh, about old times.

I got a surprise this morning, Sid visited me and believe it or not he brought me some clean pyjamas. I almost fell off my chair in surprise and he was civil. The staff brought us some tea and we chatted, we probably said more than we have in years. Then Tim Hopkins came in and we all started to talk about the old days.

At lunch time Sid went but the matron said another time he could stay for lunch. I thought that would be pushing it.

Jan 16th

Decision day do I stay or do I go? It's simple, I'm staying. Mrs Oslo came to find out my answer, when I told her she smiled, laughed and clapped her hands. She said, "You've made my day."

She asked me, "How has Sid taken your decision?"

I said to her, "that was the strange thing, when I told Sid yesterday, he got angry and left."

Mrs Oslo asked, "Does he visit often?"

And I told her, "He has come every day, after that first visit and what is more amazing, we are getting on, chatting and the like."

She looked surprised and said, "Wonders will never cease." Then she picked up her enormous file and got up to go.

"Perhaps he misses you," she said.

"No chance," I told her. "He has the house to himself now, he couldn't wait to get me out."

Dec 31st

Another year nearly over and I have been here almost a year, best decision I ever made.

As it was getting dark this evening. I was in my room thinking back over the year and I wish mum could have been here and seen me and Sid. Sid has now moved into St Peters. It turned out he was lonely and we are enjoying each other's company. I can't believe I am writing that. Mum would be so pleased. It has taken us nearly a lifetime to get on.

At tea time one of the nurses asked what our New Year's Resolution would be.

Sid said, "That's a hard one," and he winked at me. I smiled, it was good to have my brother here because some things only he and I understand.

Hope

Sister Nancy glided into the ward. The high windows allowed the light to stream in and the dust particles danced in the sunbeams. Nancy loved this work, she felt she had been born for it, to help people on the last stage of their journey which she felt was an honour.

One patient in particular worried her. He was Charles an awkward character. He shouted at the nurses and cursed them, blaming everyone but himself for his plight and yet out of everyone here, he had contributed to his situation. She heard that he had caught his leg in a mantrap, that he had set up to catch poachers.

These mantraps had been banned in England for years. He had been trapped for six hours and the resulting blood poisoning had led to him being here. When his poor wife visited him, he shouted at her and whatever she said or did never pleased him.

Today Nancy had come to visit Charles. She was not looking forward to the meeting and sent arrow prayers up to heaven as she approached his bed.

"Good morning, how are you?" she asked.

"I would feel a good deal better if you God botherers stopped trying to save my soul. I don't want to be saved, do you hear me," he said, his voice grew louder so he was almost shouting. "*I DIDN'T WANT TO BE BORN AND I DON'T, I REPEAT DON'T WANT TO BE SAVED.*"

"I hear you," said Nancy. "If I don't try to save your soul, can I sit with you?"

"If you have nothing better to do," he snarled.

So, Nancy sat and listened to his long list of grievances about his life.

"I thought you inherited and your brothers didn't." said Nancy.

"Exactly, and if I hadn't inherited, I wouldn't have set the traps to save my salmon and I wouldn't be here now, waiting to die with a bleeding nun by my bed," said Charles.

Nancy thought this was a good time to leave. As she got up, she was amazed to hear Charles say, "See you tomorrow."

And so began a daily meeting between Nancy and Charles. Nancy listened patiently and when Charles had reached the end of his moaning and started to repeat himself, Nancy reminded him she had heard it before.

"That's it then," said Charles, "that's the sum content of my life."

"Poor you," said Nancy and she left.

The next day when she visited. They sat in silence. Eventually Charles asked, "What about you then?"

"Thank you for asking," said Nancy. She told him about her early childhood and how fearful and lonely she had been. She was an only child and her parents had over protected her.

Charles listened. He didn't react or tell her not to be stupid and not to whine as he did to his wife.

Charles health was getting worse. But his manner was improving. When his wife came to visit him, he listened to her and they even held hands. Nancy was surprised, on the ward one day, she heard Charles saying sorry to his wife and even more surprised when she saw tears streaming down his face and his wife hugging him.

A few nights later Charles slipped into unconsciousness. Nancy came and sat with him and they phoned for his wife.

Nancy sat holding his hand. He came round and Nancy looked into his eyes and smiled, she asked, "Can I save your soul yet?"

He nodded and squeezed her hand. Ten minutes later he died.

Nancy bowed her head and prayed. She got up and slowly glided out of the ward. She would never forget Charles and he became for her, a reminder that there is always hope.

Variety Show

The Cupboard

If **she kept** the door very slightly ajar the moonlight from the corridor window, shone into the cupboard. Inside the cupboard she felt warm and safe, surrounded by the sheets, pillows and bedspreads stored there.

The cupboard was about six and a half feet long and two and a half feet wide. It was located at the side of a flight of stairs. Its position was ideal for Hannah as it was placed on the stairs between the kitchen and the servant's rooms, where her bedroom was.

In the day when she needed to escape, she ran up the stairs and lifted the wooden latch, the big oak door would swing open and Hannah would climb inside. She would close the door behind her and there she would let her tears fall. She longed for her home and family and to be away from the bad-tempered cook Mrs. Boil. When she heard Mrs. Boil shouting, she would come out and run down to the kitchen.

"Where have you been girl? Get down those steps and start peeling the vegetables, they won't peel themselves".

"Yes, Mrs. Boil," replied Hannah, stumbling down the stone steps to the scullery.

Hannah hated her new job as scullery maid. She

wanted to be back home with her family. At night she wanted to be tucked up in bed with her five sisters, hearing their breathing, feeling their warmth. Here she had her own room next to the cooks but it was lonely. There were strange noises, creaking and rustling and the sound of Mrs. Boil snoring. Mrs. Boil snored at night and snorted and grunted in the day, reminding Hannah of the pig her family were rearing, in the sty at the back of their cottage.

Hannah was the lowest of the servants and at twelve the youngest. She had to serve the other servants in the servant's hall. Not many of them took any notice of Hannah or even spoke to her.

Molly the parlour maid was kind though and one day she found Hannah crying as she was washing up in the shallow sink. Molly said, "don't let Mrs. Boil see you crying, she's got no sympathy but keep on the right side of her and you'll be all right."

Yet however hard Hannah tried she never seemed to get on the right side of her.

To comfort herself Hannah took food from the kitchen, when Mrs. Boil was out in the yard. She took rosy apples, slabs of fruit cake, slices of pie and anything that she thought would not be missed. She then raced up the stairs and into the cupboard.

She tucked the food under the sheets in the corner of the cupboard. On Monday she had to make sure she had it well hidden as that was wash day, when the clean sheets were needed. But they never used all the sheets, so the bottom of the cupboard was a good hiding place.

At night when Hannah heard Mrs. Boil snoring, she left her narrow bed and crept along the corridor and climbed into the cupboard. She tucked the sheets around her and then started to devour the food, whilst she ate the pain inside her stopped, only to return when all the food had gone. Then she went back to her bedroom and cried herself to sleep.

One night Hannah climbed in the cupboard, leaving the door ajar to let the moonlight in and aching with tiredness she fell asleep.

Suddenly she woke with a start. She saw the door was now open. Daylight was pouring in and an angry face was staring down at her. Hannah realized with horror that it was Mrs. Boil. She looked up at her large red face, screwed up with rage.

"Well, what have we here, then?" She bellowed, causing Hannah to almost wet herself with fear. "You've no right to be here." Then her protruding eyes fell upon the half-eaten cake by Hannah's side.

"A thief as well," she yelled, picking up the crumbling piece of cake. Hannah felt her world had stopped as she looked up at the enraged cook.

"Sorry, sorry," muttered Hannah.

"Sorry will do you no good." Shouted Mrs. Boil. "You're for it now and no mistake."

By this time the other servants had gathered and

wanted to know what was going on. Mrs. Boil put her podgy arms into the cupboard and dragged Hannah out. Hannah's feet hardly touched the ground as she was hauled down the stairs and into the kitchen. Then she was dragged down into the cellars and at the end of the corridor pushed roughly into an unused store room. Hannah heard the key being turned.

"This is what we do to thieves, you ungrateful girl." Shouted Mrs. Boil from behind the locked door. "You've only rats for company, that will teach you."

Hannah stood silently, her back against the wall and saw a small grating high up in the opposite wall, which let in a little light. She shut her eyes so she wouldn't see the rats. All she could hear was a soft scratching, was it mice or rats? Sometimes she caught the muffled sound of people's voices as they passed near the grating.

Mrs. Boil ran breathlessly to find the mistress of the house and tell her. To her disgust the mistress was more concerned for the girl's welfare than Mrs. Boil's complaints. The Mistress told the cook to return to her duties and said that she would deal with the matter. She then summoned some of the servants and questioned them closely.

Meanwhile Mrs. Boil returned to the kitchen and banged the saucepans around, muttering under her breath about the youth of today.

Hannah eventually opened her eyes and crouched down on the floor. She was scared about what would happen to her but had given up considering the possibilities as she felt she had committed the ultimate sin, stealing and she had no hope left. Would she ever get out of here?

Time stood still, it could have been one hour or ten, for Hannah had nothing to measure it by. She sat dejected and numb on the cold, cobbled cellar floor. And then she heard it. Was she dreaming? Could it be? She jumped up a flicker of hope returned. Had that really been her mother's voice, that had floated down through the grating?

Then she heard footsteps coming down the cellar corridor and the key being turned. Mrs. Boil stood there with a face like thunder.

"Come on then girl, I've been told to fetch you. Come on" and she grabbed Hannah roughly and pushed her through the cellars and up the stairs into the kitchen.

Hannah blinked in the daylight and joy of joys saw her mother. She ran to her and hugged her. Her whole body shaking with emotion as she sobbed her heart out.

"Come now lass, we're going home." said her mother "I can see this is no place for you." She glared at Mrs. Boil. "The mistress thinks the same, that she's not suited to kitchen work. She suggests Hannah gets work which allows her home each night."

Mrs. Boil was looking as if she might explode, "The mistress is going soft, she should have thrown her out without a reference."

"The mistress has given Hannah a reference and as she said to me, she's very young," replied Hannah's mother.

"I was out working at nine, straight from the orphanage," said Mrs. Boil. "And it didn't do me no harm."

"That," said Hannah's mother, "is a matter of opinion. Come on Hannah put your coat on over your gown. I'm taking you home." Holding Hannah's hand, she led her out into the courtyard, she turned to Mrs. Boil and said, "We'll collect her things later."

Hannah left the big house with the sound of Mrs. Boil grunting in discontent at the unfairness of life.

She felt such relief and joy, which increased with each step she took, as she walked away from the big house.

And the Consequence Was

Edward Huggy, the well-known psychologist was spreading golden honey on top of his homemade buttered scones. The tea table was set with bone china cups and saucers. The teapot was warming. He was ready for his guest, the renowned psychiatrist Sandra Warren.

This meeting had been planned for some time, ever since the funding had been found to combine Edward and Sandra's therapies. Both their therapies had wonderful results, in helping people overcome moderate to severe depression and it was hoped by combining them, that the resulting therapy would help even more people.

Edward had planned this informal tea, in order for Sandra and him to get to know each other and to iron out any difficulties, before they officially started working together.

The doorbell jingled and Edward opened the door to a thin tall lady, whose face was spoilt by large buck teeth set in a small mouth. Also, her ears appeared large but Edward thought this could be because she tucked her grey hair behind them, making them stick out. She wore orange trousers and a green jacket.

Edward was optimistic that although their therapies were poles apart, they would be able to come to a happy compromise.

He looked lovingly at the tea table; everything was in place. Sandra sat down on the edge of a chair. He handed her the plate of scones.

To his immense surprise, she screamed, "Get that disgusting gooey stuff away from me."

Edward quickly withdrew the plate and asked Sandra, "What's the problem?"

"Honey causes obesity," stated Sandra (at this point Edward pulled in his rotund stomach) "and horrendous tooth decay," she continued, "and sluggishness."

"I'll have you know," said Edward, who was a mild-mannered man but felt riled by Sandra's abrasive manner, "that my therapy is called the sweet treatment and kindness to the self never goes amiss."

"I'm well aware of your therapy," said Sandra, "you work with your clients to bring their problems to the surface and then, bury them. Then they ignore their problems and focus on the sweeter things of life." She sneered.

"Including honey," said Edward, "my success rate is high and my clients go on to live happy productive lives."

"Honey and hugs, isn't it," sniffed Sandra with distain, "but how long does this happy state last? My therapy actually deals with the problem, we dig it out, chew it over, lay it on the table and feel, really feel the pain."

"Ouch," said Edward.

Sandra continued, "They deal with their problems head on, none of this wishy washy, nicely does it," said Sandra.

As tea continued Edward became more and more stressed, he finished all the honey scones. If it wasn't for the funding, he would like to have shown Sandra the door and never see her again.

Sandra had similar feelings, she despaired of the high calorie, sugary foods on the tea table. She felt Edward was self-indulgent and gave people what they wanted not what they needed. She found a carrot in her bag and chewed on it miserably.

Surprisingly though, by the time they had finished tea, they had found a compromise that they were both happy with. The research would be carried out by their students, under direction from Edward and Sandra but with no need for the two of them to meet as their students would pass messages back and forth.

This is what happened and three years later the new therapy was up and running with fantastic results. It was called 'Sweet and Sour Therapy'. The first part of the therapy was to dig out and name the problem, then work to solve it, with a generous reward when each stage of the therapy was reached and an extra-large reward on completion.

Edward and Sandra received honours from the Queen for their contribution to mental health as well as for their support and mentoring of their students.

After receiving their honours at Buckingham palace Sandra and Edward were photographed together for the national papers.

Edward celebrated with friends by having a slap-up tea at the Savoy and Sandra celebrated at a vegan restaurant with her students in Soho.

Edward and Sandra never met again.

The Christmas Tree Star

Little star had been happily twinkling with mother star, when he felt a tug as if he was being pulled away from his mother's shiny safe arms.

Little star pulled back and snuggled closer to his mum. He looked up at her and said, "When I grow up, I want to be the star that the three wise men followed, to find baby Jesus."

"You can't be that star," laughed his mum, "that happened over 2000 years ago."

"Well, I want to be a famous star that people will look for in the sky, or I want to be part of the plough or the great bear constellations or something special."

"You are very special," said mother star, holding him a little tighter. "Soon it will be your turn to shine on your own, away from me, you are nearly grown up."

Little star didn't like that thought, so he stayed close to his mum and ignored the gentle tugs that became more frequent with each passing day.

Until one day he felt a huge tug and he lost hold of his mother. He was falling, falling down through inky blackness, he didn't stop until he landed with a soft thud on top of a tall Christmas tree, in Northampton Market

Square.

Little star looked around and saw children wrapped up in coats, scarfs and hats, walking with their parents who were heavily laden with parcels. A group of adults were singing little star's favourite carol, 'We Three Kings of Orient are.'

Little star forgot to miss his mum, there was so much to see. He shone brightly and people started to point and say, "What a fantastic star the Christmas tree has this year, the best ever, it's so bright." This made little star shine even more.

News of the wonderful Christmas tree star soon spread. Everyone was talking about it. Some said, "They got it from 'Poundland' its batteries will soon run out."

Others said, "The council shouldn't waste its money on buying such an expensive star."

Two people who heard about the star were Jim and Harold they were thieves. Jim said to Harold, "If we got that star, I bet we could sell it for at least a hundred pounds."

"You're right," said Harold. "Folk say it is the brightest star they have ever seen."

"Let's get it tonight," said Jim, "before someone else nicks it. We'll go after midnight when the street lights are turned off, it will be pitch black then."

But it wasn't pitch black, although all the street lights had been turned off, for little star shone even brighter in the dark.

Jim and Harold leaned their ladder against the tree. Jim held the ladder whilst Harold climbed up. He put out his hand to grab little star but the heat from little star burned his hand. He wrapped his burnt hand in his scarf.

He shouted down to Jim, "It's too hot to handle. I'll have to cut off the branch below the star and we'll get it when it falls to the ground and wrap it in our coats."

"Ok, whatever," said Jim chewing on his gum, he was getting bored. "Only get a move on, my feet are freezing."

Harold got out his Boy Scout pen knife and started hacking away at the branch that little star was caught on. As little star became free a strange thing happened, he didn't fall, instead he felt himself being pulled upwards, back up into the inky blackness.

Harold leaned forward to grab him but missed and fell off the ladder landing on top of Jim. They both lay on the ground watching as little star shot through the sky and came to a standstill high up above them.

Jim and Harold rubbed their eyes, were they dreaming? They got up, picked up their ladder and the sawn-off branch and sloped off home, throwing the branch into the river on their way. They didn't tell anyone what they had seen.

Two days later when they were watching the local news. The news reader said, "A strange occurrence happened in Northampton Market Square. The brightest and biggest Christmas tree star that the council has ever provided is missing from the towns Christmas tree, the police are investigating.

"We're for it now," said Jim.

"They can't pin anything on us, we haven't got it," said Harold.

"Shush, listen," said Jim.

The news reader continued, "A new star has been found shining over Northampton. Astronomers are puzzled as to the sudden appearance of this unknown star. The locals are calling it the missing 'Christmas tree star'.

The name stuck and people came from far and wide to see it twinkling over Northampton's market square. Jim and Harold made a fortune by setting up a market stall selling, 'Christmas-tree-star' memorabilia.

Little star twinkled extra brightly at Christmas time, when the Christmas decorations were hanging in the market square.

Sometimes he became a shooting star and would wiz back to his mum to tell her all his adventures.

"I'm very proud that you are the 'Christmas tree star,'" she said but I was proud of you anyway for being you. You have always been special and I love you this much," and she stretched out all her star points as far as they would go.

"I love you to mum but it's time to go back now."

"Yes, said mum. You really are grown up now."

As little star shot of excitedly, mother star wiped a tear from her eye. It was hard to let go.

Variety Show

Where Memories are Made

It was windy as I walked along Southwold pier. But it was not as bad as the gale that was blowing when Donald and I came here all those years ago. Then we had raced to the end of the pier.

He had run on the sheltered side protected by the shops and cafes, which were spaced at intervals, along the length of the pier. I ran on the other side, the wind lashed side, holding onto my scarf which threatened to be whipped from me. My hair was tugged by the wind and fell in chaos around my face. I reached the end of the pier first as he had become entangled with a group of pensioners, coming out of the gift shop. He ran up to me.

"At last," he said. He looked round but there was only us on this grey day at the end of the pier. He knelt down in front of me and looked straight into my eyes. "Janet, will you marry me?"

"Yes, Yes," I replied. "I thought you would never ask."

He picked me up and twirled me round. We were laughing and kissing. Then we saw a middle-aged couple who had walked up the pier, they clapped their hands and shouted congratulations.

Donald put me down and we smiled sheepishly at the couple and walked hand in hand down the pier, on the sheltered side. Beneath us the waves crashed and through the wooden slats of the floor we saw the turbulent sea.

My heart was singing with joy, I felt special, loved and secure. I loved Donald so much, he was everything to me. He made my life worth living.

That was fifteen years ago.

Yesterday I had found a letter in Donald's trouser pocket, whilst I was sorting the washing. It was crumbled but smelt strongly of perfume. I had spread it out and read it. My world turned upside down.

I felt sick and had to rush to the loo, it felt as if my insides were being stripped from me. It started to make sense. That's why he had been going on conferences for work, which he had never done before. He told me it was to ensure he got promotion, he said you have to be seen. He was spending time with her.

It was why we had become more distant but I had put it down to my work load and his, so we had less time together. But now I knew.

Suddenly all my energy left me and I slumped to the floor. I stayed there bereft, lost, and alone. Until I heard his key in the door. Then calmly I rose and on autopilot I did what I knew I had to do.

Afterwards I left and travelled here through the night. Here where my dearest dream had come true. I had loved Donald with every fibre of my being. Now I was again at the end of Southwold pier.

But I was alone and the pain was too great.

I turned and walked slowly down the pier on the sheltered side. It was then I saw the two police officers walking towards me. So, after I had passed the gift shop I crossed to the windy side of the pier, where there were two more police officers. It was on the windy, storm lashed side that they arrested me, their words torn from them by the wind.

"Janet Ross, we are arresting you for the murder of your husband Donald Ross, you do not have to say anything but anything that you do say may be taken down and used in evidence against you."

I nodded and in handcuffs I left Southwold pier.

Variety Show

Daily Life in 2060

I'm exhausted, I have been programming the robots all morning. Jerry, my husband, has no idea how hard it is. I think I have time for a quick cuppa. 'Oh no, robot gardener has bumped into robot maid. She is still trying to hang up the washing but she is putting it over his face and he has mowed over her feet and my best dress.'

I run into the garden and turn them both off, then I peg the washing up. I turn robot gardener round and switch him back on. I put robot maid onto bathroom cleaning. As I come through the kitchen door, I see robot cook putting the eggs in the mixing bowl without cracking them open. There's no point in yelling at her, I just programme her on washing up. As I enter the lounge Jessica, my two-year-old, is happily pressing buttons on the forbidden control panel and robot nanny is holding Jessica's large teddy in her steel arms and saying, "Good girl for calming down".

I scoop Jessica up, grab my car keys and slam the front door. I strap Jessica into her car seat and programme the car to take us to our local play station.

Then Jessica and I look at a 'Jane and Peter' book on basic programming for the under-fives and we sing

'How much is that doggie in the window', after we pass two robots taking some dogs for a walk. The dog's leads had got tangled around a lamp post and the robots were malfunctioning. I had to cover Jessica's ears, the language they were using was disgusting, who programmed them I wondered.

At the play station I found Susie and Janet with their toddlers. Soon the children are being entertained by the play station robots and we are able to relax and chat. As usual the talk turns to the problems of getting good robots, that do what it says on the tin.

Susie says, "Of course it's mostly men that design robots and they are not up on the subtleties of housework or childcare."

"True," says Janet. "I can't manage with these dumb robots but I can't imagine not having them."

"Our grandmothers didn't have them," I say.

"No," said Susie, "and look at them, they worked and looked after the house but they were dead by the time they were hundred, worn out poor things, complete drudges."

We all nodded at this sad fact and felt pleased that we had moved on.

Working on Empty

I'm working on empty again today.
You turn and grunt, you have it your way.
I feed the kids with irritable calm,
until it erupts and spreads its harm.
I'm working on empty and wondering why
I'm doing it again after another try,
To secure something from our fractured lives.
But having received, I know it will go,
So, I'm working on empty but you don't want to know.

Variety Show

A Fishy Tale

I never expected to be ousted by a guppy, but life is full of surprises.

Our children had left home and my husband was feeling at a loose end.

"I need a new hobby," he said, "I'm just drifting."

He decided to take up fish keeping. He started by buying all the equipment that he considered was needed. Each purchase was solemnly considered and I would be bombarded with the merits and advantages of each chosen item compared to its neighbour on the shelf. My husband became enthralled with each purchase.

At last, the great day arrived when he was to set up his fish tank. With eager anticipation he set up the aquarium. Every item was moved several times until it was in just the right position. He was really pleased with the end result.

I told him it looked good, he grunted hardly noticing my presence. On the following days I would find him standing just staring at his beloved tank.

"Are you going to get some fish then?" I asked.

"No, it's weed next," he said with sparkling eyes.

I started to realise his eyes lit up when the fish tank

was mentioned.

We went together to choose the weed. This was a mistake. I was bored after half an hour, whereas he pounded up and down the dark damp smelling rows of tanks, not speaking but obviously in seventh heaven.

On arriving home, he tried the weed in a variety of places, each time standing back and looking. Then he would shake his head, step forward and plunge his arm into the water, soaking his sleeve and slopping water out of the tank with each move. After much deliberation all was in place.

He admired his tank full of stones, wood and weed... often.

The tank took centre stage in our kitchen diner.

After a few days I said, "Are you going to get some fish now?"

"No," he replied, "the tank's environment needs two weeks to stabilise."

I considered his new hobby to be lacking in excitement but he was very pleased with what he had achieved.

Then the big day came and he brought a collection of guppies (small bright coloured fish).

Suddenly the tank became alive with darting flashes of blue and red. I started to be interested.

That tea time I noticed my husband looking at me with a loving gaze, I smiled back. He just continued to gaze. I stared at him and then realised it wasn't me he was looking at but the fish in the tank, behind my chair!

The guppies had his undivided attention. How could I compete? They were the objects of his desire, if an empty fish tank made his eyes sparkle how could I compare with an aquarium full of fish!

It was obviously unequal competition; I couldn't beat the allure of the fish so I joined my husband in watching them. It was slightly more exciting than some TV programmes.

One morning I was making my early morning cup of tea, when I noticed an extra dot in the tank. I stared, rubbed my eyes and stared again, could it be... was it...? Yes, it was a baby guppy. I was so excited; I was catching my husband's obsession.

I rushed up stairs and woke him, saying, "You're a dad."

We both ran downstairs and marvelled at this speck of creation.

The guppies produced many babies. We couldn't count them all but we loved to watch. Unfortunately, the guppies ate most of their babies. This was disheartening but worse was to follow. Tragedy struck and the fish started to die.

My husband tried to save them, not with the kiss of life but with every remedy and book he could find on the subject. He asked for advice from fellow fish keepers but nothing worked. He even had the water tested. There was nothing wrong with it.

One fish remained; our conclusion was we had a mass

murderer guppy on our hands.

This guppy lived a happy but lonely life for several months, before either committing suicide (due to remorse at his past deeds) or died due to his pampered lifestyle.

Since the death of the fish, my husband has turned his affections back to me. But yesterday I saw him with a spade, digging a pond in the middle of the lawn and mumbling something about 'bigger fish to fry'! *Help!*

Cup of Tea

He looked out of his study window at his wife lazing on the chaise lounge which she had dragged from the drawing room onto the terrace. What had he seen in her? He knew his ego had been stroked by her youth and charm. She was pretty and petite but like a fancy wrapped parcel the outer layer promised more than the gift inside. Catherine he now found to be shallow and hollow.

The book she held would not be read but glanced at, her topics of conversation were basic, surface stuff with no depth, she wanted to fritter away her life with inconsequential things. She desired designer handbags, shoes and clothes. Labels meant the world to her.

There was now no common ground between them. He longed for divorce. Divorce though would mean he would lose his beautiful family home, which had been in his family for generations. He knew she would demand her share and she had never cared for the Georgian manor they lived in. She wanted a modern home with every comfort but no character.

He looked at her, he no longer saw an object of desire but a parasite emptying him of his identity and wealth.

He got up, left his study and made his way to the kitchen he would make them both a cup of tea. How English he thought as he switched the kettle on.

Catherine loved the chaise lounge it was regal and a delight to lounge on. Surely the queen must have at least a dozen. She stroked the dark blue velvet upholstery. Edward had become a bore; she had seen some exquisite shoes in just this colour and he had quibbled over the price. He could afford it, look where they lived.

He had turned out to be mean and now kept her on an allowance as if she was a child. He spent more on the children than herself. The children were his from his first marriage, sadly his first wife had died from a stomach ulcer, poor woman. And now besides dealing with Edward she had two snotty nosed kids to deal with, thankfully they were at boarding school.

Since their marriage three years ago Edward had withdrawn from her. She felt neglected and alone and she didn't know what was wrong. They had huge rows over nearly everything but now the arguments had stopped. The silence she felt was worse and nothing of importance was ever discussed, only necessary practical matters. The only attention Edward showed her was when he made her a cup of tea, which he would drink with her and chat.

Just then Edward came out of the French doors with two cups of steaming tea. He gave her a cup and sat to the side of her on the grass drinking his.

To an onlooker they would seem the perfect couple. They discussed family matters and as always Edward quizzed her on her spending.

Then he stood up to take the cups back to the kitchen. He washed and dried them by hand as he had with his first wife. Would it look strange he wondered if both his wives died of stomach ulcers. He smiled as he hung the cups on their hooks, no he thought, for coincidences do happen.

Variety Show

A Woman's Secret

She sat upright on the hard-back chair. Her dark hair was piled high, kept in place by large kirby grips. She wore a red velvet blouse with a high collar, pinned on her blouse was a golden broach with the engraved letters SF. Her long black skirt reached to the top of her black leather boots. Her hands were placed together in her lap. She looked as if she was sitting for a portrait.

She was waiting. It was a long wait but she remained still and composed.

"Lady Lucas, Lord Wilforth will see you now," said a smartly dressed young woman.

She rose and followed her into Lord Wilforth's study. He was sitting behind a large mahogany desk.

He motioned to a straight back chair across the desk from himself. "Sit down Rose. Thank you, Judith, that is all for now. Please make sure we are not disturbed."

"Yes sir," said Judith leaving the room and quietly closing the door behind her.

Lord Wilforth looked at Rose, "Well," he said "to what do I owe the pleasure of seeing you, after all these years?"

For the first time Rose spoke.

"I hope you know I would not have come unless I had to. I understand our agreement."

"Splendid," said Lord Wilforth. "So how can I help?"

"I have been found out and I need to leave the country."

Lord Wilforth sat up, his face changed, he looked scared and angry. "You know the agreement everyone for themselves if the balloon goes up."

"I know the agreement but if I'm caught, and the net is getting closer, even now as I speak, I will spill the beans."

"You can't break the agreement," thundered Lord Wilforth banging his fist on the desk.

Rose remained composed, her voice calm as she said, "I know but they have blocked my accounts and all my assets."

Lord Wilforth's face reddened and in a threatening low voice he said, "Drat you woman. Why shouldn't I cut your throat here and now and be done with your threats?"

Rose leaned towards him. "Because," she said, "I have something you desire more than anything and money can't buy it."

"What are you talking about?"

Rose continued, "You married a barren woman didn't you Charles? You threw me over for her, for her youth, blue eyes and blonde hair. She couldn't deliver, could she? But when you dumped me, I was carrying your child, a boy, Stephen Francis." Rose reached for her brooch and rubbed the engraved initials. "Your son Charles. Only I can tell you where he is. Now will you help me?"

Charles Wilforth had gone pale. "I want proof."

"There's no time Charles, I need to leave the country now. I will send you proof. You will for once in your life have to trust someone, if you ever want to see your son."

Rose could see the dilemma in Charles's face. Eventually he reached for his cheque book and wrote out a four-figure sum. He handed it to Rose. "When you send me proof, I'll double this amount and when I see my son we'll talk again."

"*Our* son Charles, *our* son."

Rose took the cheque and stood up. "Thank you, I thought you would help." She turned and swept out of the room.

As the taxi drove Rose towards Luton airport. She took out the kirby grips and let her hair fall on her shoulders. She tapped a number into her mobile.

"Hi Sam, I've done it I have what we need. He fell for it hook, line and sinker, it was like taking candy from a baby. I'll meet you in half an hour and we will have the holiday of a lifetime."

As the taxi entered Luton airport Rose unpinned the brooch and left it on the seat. Tomorrow was another day and Rose was confident that if she had anything to do with it, nothing would stop her.

Variety Show

Anything

(A title we were given to write about at our writing group)

'Anything' is too wide,
I can't find its side.
No boundaries, hedges or gate.
I sit up uninspired until late.
I could write of a lover's tiff
Or a postman, bitten and miffed.
I could write of a pig escaping its sty
But the middle and endings pass me by.

I'd love to be inspired and know
That what I write will flow.
I'm in a delta of mud and sludge
My brain is stuck, simply won't budge.
But time ticks by and moves on
Soon the dead line, I'll come upon.
My nightmares are of, my turn to read out,
When all I have is blank paper to shout about.

So please forgive me, can't you see
'Anything' is not for me.
I need a guide, a sign, a way
To help my writing block to sway,
Removing itself from my mind.
A different title would be kind.
My days then won't be so fraught
And I could write as I ought.

So, my fellow writing chums
This title is why I've looked so glum.
But now my friends I've done my bit
And yes … **this is it!**

Variety Show